CYCLO-✕-CROSS

2nd Edition

BY SIMON BURNEY

VELOPRESS • BOULDER, COLORADO

ACKNOWLEDGMENTS

The author would like to express his gratitude to Martin Seddon for his help and cooperation with the technique photos, also to Martin Eadon for his input into the training section.

Library of Congress Cataloging-in-Publication Data

Burney, Simon.
    Cyclo-cross : training & techniques / by Simon Burney. --2nd ed.
        p.   cm.
    Includes index.
    ISBN 1-884737-20-X
    1. Bicycle motocross--Training.   2. Winter sports.   I. Title.
    GV1049.3.B87   1996
    796.6'2--dc21   96-37531
                                                                                 CIP

Photography on pages: 2, 3, 12, 63, 73, 80, 94, 129, 134, 144, 145, 146, 149 by
    John Pierce/Photosport Intl.
Photography on pages: 30, 48, 52, 57, 64, 65, 72, 81, 83, 95, 124, 143 by Cor Vos
Photography on pages: 17, 19, 23, 28, 33, 40, 49, 51, 53, 55, 56, 58, 59, 61, 67,
    69, 70 by Dave Bull
Cover photo of Alison Dunlap by Casey B. Gibon
Back cover photo of Richard Groenendaal by Cor Vos
Cover and Interior Design by Erin Johnson

VeloPress™ • 1830 N. 55th Street • Boulder, Colorado 80301-2700 • USA
TEL: 303/440-0601 • FAX: 303/444-6788 • E-Mail: velopress@7dogs.com
Web Site: www.velocatalogue.com

TO PURCHASE ADDITIONAL COPIES OF THIS BOOK
OR OTHER VELOPRESS™ BOOKS, PLEASE CALL 800/234-8356.

CONTENTS

INTRODUCTION

WHAT IS CYCLO-CROSS?

All cyclists have heard of it. Even your average "man in the street" knows it has something to do with running around a muddy field with a bike on your back, because that is the bit they remember from the clip they saw on television. But cyclo-cross has remained a bit of a mystery to all but the committed for too long.

Basically, cyclo-cross is the winter branch of bicycle racing; it takes place off-road, in parks, woods and fields. Anyplace with enough space to create a lap of one or two miles (that's 1.6km to 3.2km) can be used for 'cross. Circuits vary tremendously from place to place, but all comprise similar features: terrain which calls for bike-handling skills, strength and speed; and, of course, sections which are unrideable and force the riders to run with their bikes.

Race distances vary depending on the terrain, but race duration is pretty much standard: 30 minutes for juveniles (12-15 years), 40 minutes for juniors (16-18 years), and 60 minutes for seniors (over 18). Women race for a similar time; 50 minutes is optimum.

All racing is controlled by the national cycling federation of the particular country, or a cyclo-cross association affiliated to the national federation. The UCI (Union Cycliste Internationale) controls the sharp end of the sport: the World Cup and world championships.

More about them later.

The racing season starts in early September, with events every week-end until mid-February, but numbers of races vary from country to country. For instance, in Great Britain, where small, local events are popular, there were 220 races listed in the 1995-96 season handbook. In Switzerland, where there is just one major race a weekend that everybody rides, there were fewer than 30 total.

So, how did the sport develop? Cyclo-cross started as an organized form of cycle sport in the early part of the 20th century, and was looked upon as good winter training for the road season; it was a lot of fun, and a great way for cyclists to keep fit. It still is, of course, but over the years it has developed into more of a sport in its own right.

The first world championships were held in Paris in 1950. Interest continued to grow, and in 1967 it became necessary to divide the championships into amateur and professional events. The amateur and professional championships remained separate until 1995, when the whole of cycle sport became "open" and an open championship was held, with a supporting "espoirs" race for riders under 23 years of age.

In its first year, the espoirs race was just a European championship, but it was upgraded to full world status in 1996 ... the same year a demonstration juvenile world championships was held. In the near

A typical sight on a winter afternoon somewhere in darkest Europe ... below freezing temperatures, but a crowd still shows up to watch the stars compete.

Even the minor 'cross nations occasionally turn out a quality rider. In Britain's case, it is Roger Hammond, world junior champ and hopeful star of the future.

future, don't be surprised to see this become more than just a demonstration, and be joined by a women's title race, to fall in line with similar road and mountain bike events.

Today, cyclo-cross is still one of the most popular winter sports in countries such as Switzerland and Belgium. Although in certain European countries the number of races has fallen slightly, the big events still draw crowds of up to 30,000 spectators. And world championships have grown in popularity in recent years.

The big draw for the spectators are the handful of well-paid 'cross specialists who compete in something like 35 races a season. Many of these have either given up lucrative road-racing careers to concentrate their efforts on 'cross, or complement their summer-season mountain bike or road racing by competing 10 months a year. Belgium and the

Netherlands can boast up to 20 races a weekend, all attracting the local star riders, as well as crowd-drawing road stars who are well paid to pad out the field and put on a show for knowledgeable audiences brought up on a diet of cycle racing.

In some countries, such as the United States and Great Britain, the sport will probably never reach these heights. But there has been a steady, significant increase in the numbers of races and participants since the appearance of the mountain bike in our lives. Suddenly, off-road riding and racing have transformed all branches of cycle sport, introducing massive changes in bike technology, bike sales, and cycling as a leisure activity. Racing off-road is a cool thing to do, and cyclo-cross has benefited enormously.

For the serious rider, the ultimate aim is to become world champion. But along the way, there are races and competitions at every level — local, national and international. These also give summer road and mountain bike racers the chance to prepare and improve their fitness and bike-handling skills with regular training in cyclo-cross events at whatever level they choose.

In general, cycle sport has become a 12-month-a-year occupation. No longer do summertime racers take long rests during the winter months, while 'cross riders rest in the summer; each takes part in the other's events in order to improve their abilities, as levels of fitness improve generally.

If serious competition is not your scene, it is no reason to avoid 'cross. It can be ridden at any level and provides an enormous amount of fun — and that is what sport is all about! ■

CHAPTER I

GETTING STARTED

Normally, the first step to take on your way to racing 'cross would be to get involved with a cycling club that already has members competing. It is possible to go it alone and join your national federation as an individual, but by doing it all through a club, you will be exposed to all sorts of good advice and benefits that will help speed your progress. If you can find a club or team in your local area that has an interest in 'cross, then so much the better. Perhaps they already promote a race or have a team that travels together to races. Whatever the case, if you can get involved with somebody who knows about 'cross, it will save you a lot of time organizing everything on your own.

If you are unsure about finding a club, contact your national cycling federation, which will give you a list of clubs in your area. If there is a national cyclo-cross association where you live, they will be most informed about cyclo-cross clubs in your area. Failing that, try your local bike shop; they usually know what is going on locally. While you are there, invest in a helmet if you don't already own one. That and a bike are all you need to show up at a race — chances are you already own a bike!

If you intend competing in any large races, or competing abroad, you will need a racing license. This is the same as is required for road racing, so if you are already competing, you will have one; if not, get one anyway — then you can race during the summer as well.

Next on the list: Find some races. Again, try the bike shop; they are likely to know what is going on, and may be showing a poster or two advertising forthcoming events.

Also, national federations usually issue a complete calendar at the beginning of the winter season. In the U.K., this comes in the form of a handbook that not only lists the races, but also all the rules and regulations of racing, along with other useful information.

Once the season is under way, a 'cross specialty magazine will list the upcoming events. But remember that not all races offer race-day registration; some need pre-entering up to three weeks in advance.

Converting a road bike

Let's assume you have joined a club, have a helmet and know where the races are; all you are missing is a bike. Chances are you will not have a specially built 'cross machine just yet. If you do, then read no further. But to be honest, until you have tried the sport and decide you like it and want to continue, then you are probably better off adapting an old road bike — maybe your training or winter bike — before buying more specialized equipment.

With a standard road bike, there are a few modifications you can do to make life a little easier. But with standard road-frame clearances, you are going to be very limited in what you can do about problems caused by mud clogging everything up on bad-weather days. Only a change of frame can solve that problem.

The first thing to improve is traction. Traction is relatively easy to achieve by fitting 'cross tires with plenty of grip. If your wheels are fitted with sprint rims for tubulars or sew-ups, then the choice of relatively cheap rubber is not vast, but you should be able to find a studded tire for the rear wheel, and a similar, smaller stud for the front. These will suffice for any conditions you should encounter, and at this stage there is no need to change tires for different course conditions.

You will need lower gears to cope with the slower speeds, harder terrain, and other obstacles common to 'cross. Assuming you have a double chainset, the best and cheapest way to alter this is to simply change the cluster of cogs on the back wheel.

Most standard chainsets come fitted with 42/52 chainrings; if you have a 39-tooth inner ring, that is perfect. Leave the big ring on the outside and adjust your front derailleur as close as you can to it to keep your chain on, though you will probably be using only the inner ring to race on initially.

For the cogset at the back, use something like a 12- or 13-28. Check to be sure that your rear derailleur can cope with the 28-tooth cog (most can), and check the chain length. Better still, fit a new chain.

This will give you as wide a range of gears as you will need just by using the inner ring. With the new big cog on the back, anything you cannot ride you will have to run. You will be amazed how much more you will be able to ride as your fitness and technique improve, so don't worry if at first you seem to be off the bike as much as on it!

Next thing to change are the pedals. Chances are you have some kind of clipless road set-up — Look, Time, Shimano or something similar — and road shoes to match. You know how slippery these can be just walking out of the house to go on a training ride, so racing 'cross with them is going to be an adventure, to say the least! If you own a mountain bike, rob the pedals off that and use the matching shoes. Otherwise, invest in a pair of off-road clipless pedals and shoes. Make sure they are double-sided pedals, as single-sided just take too much time to enter and exit.

Shift levers for 'cross used to be found in the ends of handlebars ... then, technology brought us Shimano's STI and Campagnolo's Ergopower, which are perfect for 'cross bikes. If you are still on down-tube shifters, then you will need to change, either to the above, or to bar-end shifters. What you do not want to do is take your hands off the bars to shift gears on rough ground.

The brake lever/gear lever combos permit you to shift on impulse, very quickly and in the right position, which is perfect because 'cross racers spend so much time with their hands on the brake levers. Bar-end shifters come a close second, with just a slight change of position to shift gears, and with quite a weight savings, which is not to be ignored. In the end, it comes down to what you have available or can afford; the choice is yours!

You will be stuck with the brake calipers you have, as they will be suited to the frame's clearances. But if you are running an economy model, then I advise upgrading the brake pads, something better suited to the rims you intend using. And make sure they are well adjusted — you will need to slow down effectively!

Adjust your position on the bike very slightly from your normal road position to give you better control on rough ground and help with the initially awkward mounts and dismounts. Lower the saddle, no more than 1cm, and raise the handlebars a similar amount. Next time you re-tape your handlebars, raise the brake levers a touch to give a more upright position. You will be riding on the brake levers a lot, so make sure you are comfortable.

Once you have replaced your tires, pedals and shift levers, and adjusted your position, brakes and front derailleur, your old bike will be fine to get you started. If you catch the 'cross bug and go for a specially built bike, you can easily return your old bike to its original state, or use it for a spare race bike or training machine.

Converting a mountain bike

Even the most committed "roadie" now has a mountain bike hidden away in the depths of the garage, and this is likely to be the machine that comes out when the urge to get on the start line of a 'cross hits. Built for off-road use, the mountain bike has all the basic requirements. And with a few refinements, you can put together a nice, fast bike.

Start with the frame. There isn't a whole lot you can do with this, but take off any surplus accessories, such as bottle cages, reflectors, racks, etc. If you have suspension front or rear, either replace it with a rigid alternative, which will also lighten the bike, or at least adjust it to make it as "hard" as possible.

Now turn your attention to the wheels. Fit the narrowest tires you can find; normally, 1.5-inchers are readily available. These will provide a lower rolling resistance and increase the mud clearance. If you have a selection of cogs at your disposal, go with a standard 12-28 instead of 12-32, and drop off the inner chainring. You won't need it, and it jut adds weight and a place for more crud to accumulate.

The rest of the bike can pretty much stay as is. You could add a set of dropped bars, but this is quite a major ordeal — to do this would mean a new stem, bar, brake lever/shifters and riding position. It may be best to leave the bike with straight bars for now and replace them later, or wait, save up for a 'cross frame, transfer some components, and use dropped bars on that!

Acquiring a coach

One of the best steps you can take as a young rider, or as someone new to 'cross, is to get yourself hooked up with a coach. An experienced coach will be able to help you through the complex area of training and training schedules. And you will find it enormously beneficial just to have someone to talk to who knows the sport.

Your coach does not have to have been a top rider, though obviously some race experience is handy. There are even top coaches around who have never raced, but nonetheless have the ability to communicate and get the best out of riders. You must be able to tell all your thoughts, feelings and worries to this person, and you must be able to trust him or her implicitly.

Most federations have lists of coaches, but 'cross specialists are a rare breed. If your federation has an affiliated 'cross association, look there. Cyclo-cross coaching schemes are in operation, and someone with this qualification will be the best person to approach. Chances are they are already qualified as road or track coaches, too, which is a bonus. Try to find someone in your area, as you will need to see them on a regular basis. But talk to as many people as you can, and find someone you can get along with easily. When you find the right person, you will know!

Season planning

As a rule, the 'cross season runs from early September to mid-February, with races every weekend. The major races in the calendar usually stick to the same weekends each year, and the national- and world-championship dates are fixed by the UCI.

Internationally, the World Cup season gets under way in mid-October, around the same time as most countries' opening major race or national-series event. By the end of October and into November, things are heating up, the road season is long gone, and everyone intending to race has started his or her season by now.

For Europeans, December and a glut of racing around the holiday season sees riders trying to come to form for the second weekend in January at their national championships, which for most countries also serves as the world-championship selection race. The United States, however, holds its nationals in early December, which can make the U.S. season quite a short, intense affair.

The World Cup finals come the last weekend in January, one or two weekends before the world's in early February, with a couple of weekends' racing after that to show off the new rainbow jersey — or exact revenge on the guy wearing it!

Between all the major dates, small races and series abound, and it is with these that you should start racing. A lot of smaller races are held on Saturdays, giving the regular 'cross riders a good warm-up for a major race on Sunday, and the road riders an excellent training session and Sunday free for a club run or training on the road.

Cyclo-cross for the roadie

Cyclo-cross is an ideal winter activity for the summer road racer, for a number of reasons. As an aid to improved bike handling it cannot be beaten; after a winter riding 'cross, the problems of bad road surfaces, racing in the rain and descending will be a lot easier to cope with, as 'cross teaches you how to race and handle your bike properly in all conditions.

Given the efforts required in a 'cross race — not to compete at a high level but just simply to get around the course — there is no better way to train than by supplementing the normal winter training of a road racer with occasional competitive outings off-road. 'Cross requires great strength, agility and cardiovascular fitness, and these are all qualities that road riders try to develop during the winter months. Long, steady distance work on the road bike, regular stretching and running, plus circuit training, are all used to a great extent anyway; these should be continued, but with the addition of 'cross, which adds the competitive element to keep you going.

If the weather is bad for long periods, it sometimes becomes dangerous to go out on the roads, and very uncomfortable in cold weather. But an hour's 'cross is equivalent to a two- or three-hour road ride — plus, you avoid the icy roads, keep warm and still get in a high-quality training session.

Continental road riders have always used 'cross more than their British or American counterparts, even at the very highest levels. One of the all-time greats, Bernard Hinault, was a real fan of 'cross and used it regularly as part of his winter preparation, claiming it provided complementary training and taught riders to improvise, as they never knew what surface they would have to ride on.

A cyclo-cross race anywhere in Europe will always attract a good turn-out of road riders, and while it is true that many of the stars are paid good money to show up because they attract big crowds, they are still all there for a purpose — to prepare for the summer.

If you doubt the worth of replacing your traditional Sunday training ride with a cyclo-cross race, then race the smaller Saturday races instead. They are usually lower-key affairs, and this will leave your Sunday free for your normal training on the road.

And don't just *race* on the 'cross course; it is well worth putting one day a week aside to train on it, too. You will usually find some organized 'cross training going on one evening a week somewhere close by. Don't worry about involving yourself with the interval training that the specialists use; just simply go for a ride for a minimum of one hour, and use the session as a guide to your fitness — I'll bet it makes you gasp!

Assuming you have ridden a full road summer season through to September, start riding 'cross during November. This will give you a good break from competitive cycling, and avoid any staleness creeping in. You should continue doing your usual winter work and continue riding through to early February. This then gives you the rest of February and March to get used to the longer distances required for the road, but with quality sessions already "in the bank."

Cyclo-cross for the mountain bike racer

A whole new breed of cyclist has evolved over the past few years. Today, there are people racing off-road before they have even discovered road bikes and road races — people for whom riding in the dirt is all they have ever known, or ever want to know! But as with road racing, mountain bike races have established a season which runs from February through to October leaving the winter months barren to those wishing to compete.

Today's mountain bike stars still go back to their roots when they want to have some fun! Tim Gould started life on a 'cross bike and still finds time to win races during the winter, despite being one of the truly great mountain bike riders during the summer.

Now, name me a handful of Euro' mountain bike stars who do not come originally from a 'cross background! For the likes of Thomas Frischknecht, Henrik Djernis, David Baker and Daniele Pontoni, 'cross was all they ever knew. Suddenly, along came mountain bikes, and like the proverbial ducks to water, they took to it and never looked back.

Cyclo-cross gives mountain bike racers the edge, no doubt about it. This edge comes mainly from the added bike-handling skills required, the extra speed, plus the extra fitness gained from training 11 months a year instead of just seven. The other benefits are in line with those gained by road riders.

In many countries it is possible to race 'cross on a mountain bike, more so in the States than anywhere else, and initially this is fine, as it reduces the outlay of expense on extra machinery. But the real advantage will come from racing a 'cross bike during the winter, then switching to a mountain bike in the summer. On a "proper" 'cross course, a 'cross bike should be the faster option, both for riding and for carrying. This increased speed develops new skills and faster reflexes that are subsequently transformed to the mountain bike when spring rolls around.

Certainly, there will be occasions during the winter when a mountain bike, with its variation on position, traction and gearing, is the right choice for certain races. And there are no rules, except at world championships and category A races, barring the use of this bike (and even then it is only simply a matter of wheel size).

But for the majority of your racing, you will benefit greatly from experience on a 'cross bike. The main advantages you will see come summertime are a faster race start; greater confidence when racing in close quarters with other competitors; improved skill in dismounting for obstacles, covering unrideable sections on foot with the bike shouldered, and mounting afterward; and being more relaxed and in better control at faster speeds.

Specializing

There will come a time when you may suddenly realize that 'cross is for you, and is a sport you would like to concentrate on. As you will see in later chapters, a top 'cross rider today competes 10 months a year, and summer racing, be it road or mountain bike, is a vital part of the preparation.

If you are a relative beginner eager to do well at 'cross, you should go straight into the year plan in the training section. But if you have started life using the summer as your target season, you will have to adapt your usual plan somewhat to cater for the different needs of 'cross.

If you are used to competing from March to September, and then taking five months off, it is a big change to increase to a season that includes racing from April to August/September, and again from October to February. So it is vital to increase your rest time during the season.

You will find you will go as well during the summer as you did when you were a road specialist, and for several reasons. You will be fitter longer, and that is bound to rub off. You will be training longer than you are used to, and you will be resting more effectively if you follow the advice and build your training in stages followed by rest periods.

Most people who are just riding a summer season tend to train from January 1, start racing around March 1, and finish in July because they are fed up — though "stale" is a better term. Because they are so keen, they train hard from the New Year, usually in grim weather, start racing as soon as they can, and never take a break — and if the body can take it, the mind cannot. So they finish their season early and plan to have a really good crack the next season; they train really hard all winter long, and then the same thing happens!

A 'cross specialist, on the other hand, will not be racing until April, when the weather is probably better. They have a steadier start into the season, and will still be keen and reaching a peak in July and August when the big races and major objectives come up, and when the weather is nice. The advantages of winter racing rub off during the summer, too.

One of the biggest changes you go through during the summer is one of attitude. Because you know that the road races are merely a stepping stone to greater things in the winter, it takes a certain amount of pressure off, and with less pressure it is surprising how many riders end up performing better!

Race promotion for the first-timer

Tired of having to travel to find races? Or maybe you think you could do a better job than the guy who put on the last race you rode. There can never be too many races on the calendar, and a 'cross is probably the easiest kind of bike race to promote, so collect some friends and put on a race.

All the big races out there started small, so follow suit. Race organizers have to grow with their events, so start with a Saturday-afternoon affair for the locals, and before you know it you could be staging the national championships!

First off, find a venue. This could be the park you train in, your kids' school playground, or the woods behind the local trash dump ... anywhere with a variety of ground that will let you set out a circuit of one or two miles. But if your site has a few facilities attached to it, then so much the better. Sports centers and schools are favorite locations. They have changing facilities, rooms to use as headquarters for registration and results, larger rooms for prize presentations and parking for the hordes of competitors and spectators that will show up! The grounds of these buildings usually also comprise grassland, steep banks, asphalt paths and rougher ground that will suit a race circuit. The only other requirement is a little imagination.

A boring piece of grassy meadow can be transformed with a few steel pins and a length of marking tape; if your race venue cannot help out with this stuff, then ask the local authority or construction company for a loan of equipment.

If there are enough natural obstacles around to force the riders off their bikes six to 10 times a lap — over logs, up short, steep run-ups, over a ditch, and so on — then leave your course as is. If the area you choose is relatively free of anything but grass, then you are going to have to construct some obstacles. Make them no higher than 15.75 inches (40cm); wide enough to allow two riders across side-by-side; and solid enough so that if they are rideable, they will not collapse if hit or stepped on. Also, mark them tightly on each side so that they cannot be ridden around.

Play around with the location of these hurdles. Put some at the bottom of slopes to make them into run-ups; put others out on their own to let the skillful bunny-hoppers make up time, and group some together in twos or threes to create some flat running sections.

Mark out a pit area, preferably on a running section and near a water supply, with an area on the right side of the circuit wide enough to accommodate mechanics and spare bikes.

For the start area, either find a wide, flat piece of ground that will allow the riders to start in one long line, or find a long road section that leads into the circuit proper. Try to allow the field time to spread out before they hit the first obstacle or bottleneck; riders really hate queuing on the opening lap, believe me!

At your finish line, allow room for results judges, and provide some cover if possible ... results sheets drenched in rain do not make for easy reading. And if the finish can be down a barriered road, then so much the better for spectators, sprint finishes and photographers.

Don't forget when setting out the course that it is a cyclo-cross, not a mountain-bike race. The emphasis should be on the speed, skill and strength of the rider. Do not include any extended sections of single-track, as it causes too many problems with lapped riders; avoid extreme climbs or descents that favor the attributes of a suspended mountain bike; and skip sections of ground that will turn your 'cross into a foot race if the rains arrive.

Once you have figured out the location, circuit and course design, try not to keep it a secret; take it to the people. The major difference between a race in Belgium and a race in the United States is the number of people who show up to watch, and most of this is due to the location of the race. A race in Belgium will usually start and finish in the town or village, or at least in a city-center park area, which almost guarantees some spectators. All too often races get put out in the sticks with one man and a dog watching. If you can get the right venue to attract a crowd, you will find it easier to get local businesses involved in sponsorship; your race will grow, and everybody benefits. ■

CHAPTER 2

EQUIPMENT

The cyclo-cross bike

Until the early 1990s, the modern 'cross bike had been developing nicely in line with the current trends on road bikes. The serious competitor rode on new components and frames; those using 'cross as a winter training diversion simply changed a few bits around on the winter bike, using cast-offs from the road bike, and raced on frames more suited to carrying fenders and touring baggage.

A modern 'cross bike.....

Then, suddenly, the bicycle industry in general, and component manufacturers in particular, experienced massive change as the technical revolution that was the mountain bike appeared. Within a few years, bike-component design radically altered not so much how a bike looked, but how effectively it worked and how much it weighed.

Gone are the days when 'cross riders used gas-pipe tubing for frames, 40-spoke wheels "for strength," brake levers with cables coming out of the top, and toeclips and straps. Modern technology means new materials for frames and wheels that allow less weight and greater strength, gear changing without the need to change hand position, step-in pedal systems and new tire technology.

And nowadays, it's never just the one bike at a race; the modern 'cross rider is rarely seen without two bikes, or sometimes three, as the problem of mud interfering with components means regular changes of machine. Efficient and regular bike changing are now an important part of your game plan — races can be won or lost over the time it takes to clean out a pedal!

The following sections cover how to go about building the perfect 'cross bike, and you will find that a lot more thought and preparation is required than for a road machine. Fads in equipment come and go; technology is still playing a fast-moving part in what is available; and ideas change. So it is important to keep your eyes open at races and see what is being used, especially among the top guys. Road stars can be paid big money to use something they don't particularly like. But the top 'crossmen usually use equipment they feel happiest with, and it is certainly not a case of "the most expensive is best."

The frame

After frame size, the most important choice to make when buying a new frame is the material it is to be made from. This will be governed to some extent by the amount of money you are willing to spend. Steel, aluminum, carbon fiber, titanium, metal matrix composite ... blame the mountain bike if the choices make your head spin!

On the road, thin-walled alloy frames have been accepted cautiously due to their certain lack of rigidity. But in 'cross, the alloy frame

The front derailleur pulley on an Alan frame shown here routes the cable from the top tube/seat tube route, back up into a regular bottom-pull derailleur.

rules the roost, and the aluminum alloy frame made by Alan in northern Italy is the "winningest" 'cross frame to date. Since their introduction in the late 1970s, Alan frames have been the choice of the world's leading riders, and although competitors to the builders from Saccolongo come and go, the probability is high that the guy who won your last race was riding one.

The one big advantage of any alloy or composite frame bought off-the-shelf is that it will almost certainly have the correct geometry, adequate mud clearance, and all the right bits in all the right places. Another plus is the weight advantage over certain steel frames, of which only the lightest can compete. And the relatively thick walls of alloy are more resilient to knocks or crash damage than a steel frame of similar weight. Also, being a softer material, alloy is ideal for absorbing shock and can give a comfortable ride on the roughest of ground. And, as your mechanic will tell you, the easy-clean, anodized finish looks good all season, and cuts down your cleaning time on Sunday evening!

Enough praise of alloy ... there are some downsides to alloy, and some advantages to a custom-built steel frameset. The main disadvantage to alloy is its relatively short life in comparison to steel. The frame gradually grows softer, and after a couple of seasons should be demoted to a training bike, whereas, if you are lucky, a steel frame will last a couple of seasons longer. Should you break an alloy frame, repair is not straightforward, as the importer is usually able to carry out only small repairs; anything major will have to go back to the manufacturer.

The final problem is price. These frames are by no means cheap, and if you are looking at buying two or three identical bikes, then the outlay can be considerable.

Steel frames come in a vast array of tubing types, shapes, sizes, weights and prices, and no amount of advice here can replace an afternoon talking to a good framebuilder. A good builder will listen to your requirements and advise you on size, dimensions and which tubing is suitable for your weight and style of riding.

But beware: There are still plenty of builders around with next to no experience of a modern 'cross frame, and you may find yourself leaving the shop with something resembling a touring frameset with cantilever brakes on. Try to find someone who is building frames for established riders, and you will be on the right track.

Tubing varies greatly, but tubesets suitable for 'cross come from Reynolds (531, 653; 753 is an all-time great), Columbus (SLX, MAX), Tange, Dedacciai, and Ishiwata. For an all-around good value, a classic tubing like Reynolds 531 or its equivalent from one of the above combines excellent strength and a good life span; the rest is in the hands of the builder. Complete the frame with good-quality lugs; a wide-ish fork crown to give adequate front-wheel clearance; and short rear drop-outs. Avoid vertical drop-outs, as these mean that the wheel cannot be moved easily between the chainstays, should this be required.

If you have a frame custom built, the geometry should be discussed at length with the builder. But as a general guide, you should look for a top tube and seat tube both 1cm shorter than on your road bike; a slightly shallower seat angle to put a little more weight over the back wheel; and slightly longer chainstays. Have the builder leave out the chainstay bridge, to allow the mud picked up by the rear wheel to clear more easily. The bottom bracket should also be slightly higher to give a little more pedal clearance.

Brazed-on fittings should include cantilever brakes front and rear, and cable stops to route the rear brake cable along the top of the top tube — either covered cable all the way along, or a single stop at the front of the top tube, then a seat-lug guide to route bare cable to the brake.

Gear-cable routing is a matter of personal preference. I prefer cable stops on the bottom head lug and cables under the bottom bracket shell, but the current trend is to send everything along the top tube, with the rear cable going down the right-hand seat stay into the rear derailleur; the front cable going down the seat tube, either into a top-pull front derailleur, or around a small pulley wheel and back up into a regular-pull front derailleur. This trend is to keep the down tube, where mud is thrown off the front wheel, free of cables. But the route across the top tube means slightly longer cables ... and it doesn't look so nice! Once you have decided on positioning of cable stops, request split stops that allow the removal of cables without disconnecting derailleurs to allow easy lubing of inner cables.

The frame should be finished off with a good-quality headset, often overlooked but vital to the ride. A headset that is loose or worn will rattle on bumpy descents and adversely affect braking; too tight a headset will affect steering and general balance. Go for a sealed unit — the obvious choice is Shimano, followed closely by Campagnolo.

Wheels

The most important component on the bike is undoubtedly the wheel/tire combination. Until recently, the choice was pretty simple: Pick suitable rims, hubs and spokes; find a good wheel builder to make the components into a finished article; and go race 'em. Then along came composite wheels developed for road and triathlon racing, plus new deep-rim technology for regular spoked wheels, and our once-simple choice was turned into more sleepless nights ... which to go for?

Spoked wheels first. They're still the choice of the majority until the price of the new stuff comes down to make them affordable to all. The difference between a good pair and an average pair does not come down to the components they are made up with — it comes down to the building. Just as a good framebuilder will make a difference to your frame, so a working relationship with a good wheel builder will mean well-constructed wheels to start with, and constant care throughout the season.

Small-flanged hubs are a must, as are stainless spokes. They require more attention at the building stage, as they tend to stretch more than chrome, but after that you should never encounter broken spokes, and you will certainly appreciate the easy cleaning that stainless provides.

Again, with recent hub developments, quality comes cheaply nowadays; most hubs have good-quality sealed bearings, and can be rebuilt onto new rims as they wear out.

The main choice you will have to make is the type of rim and number of spokes. The better-quality rims you use, the fewer spokes you can gamble on, with the resultant weight savings. Unless you are particularly heavy on equipment, 32 spokes are most suitable. Light riders can use 28 front and rear, or 28 front/32 rear. I've known riders to use 24-spoke wheels, tied and soldered, without any trouble. They certainly save a lot of weight.

You can skimp on spokes only if you are using a good-quality rim, and of the regular-style rims Mavic is the name to go for. The GP4 is undoubtedly the best quality/value rim on the market and has been tried and tested for years now. V-section rims are just great for 'cross; originally intended for time-trial use, they are immensely strong and very easy to clean during a race.

At this stage, you must decide whether you are going to race on tubular tires (sew-ups) or clinchers. Most rim types are available in both varieties, but usually as different model names. Until recently there would have been no choice — you would always have raced on tubulars — but tire development has moved on, and now clinchers are probably more common. The prime disadvantage of the clincher rim is that the rim walls into which the tire fits are not as strong as the box section on a tubular tire rim, and thus are more susceptible to dents.

The next step up the wheel ladder is to use regular spoked wheels, but with deep-section rims. These are a real improvement: lighter and stronger, they also track better in deep mud or sand, as the mud or sand does not cover the rim and force the spokes to cut through it. They are available either in regular 28/32 holes to lace onto regular hubs, or you can buy pre-built wheel packages with as few as 16 spokes. Campagnolo leads the field here — Shamals is the original model the company introduced, but now there is a complete range, including a slightly heavier clincher model at a budget price. Other makes to look for are HED, FIR, Corima and the Mavic Cosmic.

The name on the fastest tire, mounted on the fastest wheel! The ultimate pairing of a Dugast tubular on a Spinergy wheel.

At the top of the heap is the composite wheel. Made from carbon fiber, they come in a variety of designs, most based on the three- or four-spoke principle. All have the advantage of a deep section that cuts through loose ground; the majority are rigid and light (although some of the cheaper ones are heavier than a regular spoked wheel); and all are easily cleaned.

The undoubted market leader for 'cross is the Spinergy wheel. A unique design in carbon fiber, the Spinergys use a regular alloy rim as their braking surface, and are very light. They are also available in both tubular and clincher versions. At the 1996 world championships in Paris, seven of the top 10 finishers — including two of the medalists — used these wheels.

Other makes to look out for are Specialized, FIR, and Corima. Try to find the ones that have an alloy braking surface; the laws of physics see to it that braking on carbon in wet mud is not too efficient!

The disadvantages of all composite wheels are damage repair and price. If you start knocking chunks out of the carbon, they aren't going to last long, and if they go out of true you cannot do much with a spoke key! Prices are high, especially if you are outfitting two or three bikes, so if you are lucky enough to lay your hands on some, treat them with care and save them for the big occasions.

Tires

As mentioned in the previous section, the swing from tubular tires to clinchers has meant that the availability of certain models is sketchy depending on where you live and who you know. The specialized 'cross-equipment market has never been huge, and shops are not willing to invest in a big range of tires if they sell only a dozen a year. This means that what may be the best just isn't available, so shop around and if you get lucky, buy as many as you can afford — you may never find them again!

The main reasons for the recent popularity of clinchers are their increased availability and simple economics. If you flat on a clincher, unless you actually split a sidewall or put a hole in the casing, it is going to be cheap to repair or replace the inner tube. If you do the same on a tubular, replacing and resticking it is an expensive, time-consuming operation.

That said, in my opinion, the ride offered by a tubular is far superior to that of a clincher, and in 90 percent of situations, big races are still going to be won on a glued-on tire. Fat clinchers offer their biggest advantages on very rocky or icy ground, or during training, when they are simple to repair if you should flat. Otherwise, they simply do not ride as well as a tubular.

Now that fatter tires are available, the choice dependent upon the race circuit can be bewildering. Not only do you need to decide which tread pattern is suitable, but also which size to use. As a general rule, if you are using the same wheels and tires for all conditions, go for something in the 28-32mm range. Most clinchers come in this size, and best of these is the Specialized Tri-Cross 35mm (which is actually under-sized). But also look for Tioga Greyhound, IRC, Ritchey and Vredestein.

Don't forget to use an inner tube that is compatible in size to the clincher tire you are using. Do not be tempted to use road tubes as these are too narrow and will have to stretch too much to fill the space, so fit a 28-35mm tube.

If you decide to race on tubulars, then the choice with a fatter section is more limited. Most are around 24mm and these include Barum, Vittoria and Wolber.

As far as tread patterns are concerned, go for a small, square stud pattern for the front wheel (Barum G11, Vittoria Mastercross, Clement Leopard), and an arrow shape or larger stud design for the rear wheel (Wolber Cross 28, Barum G19, G12, Clement Griffo, Vittoria Tigre). In most circumstances, what you use depends on what you can find, but all of the above are suitable for all race conditions.

When you are at a stage in your racing where national titles or world's selection are looming, then it is time to become more specialized in the tires you choose for different conditions. The choice most definitely makes a difference.

Eighty percent of the bikes at the 1996 world championships sported a tubular tire made by Dugast. These are hand-made in France, incredibly light and fast, and available in sizes from 28-40mm. Unfortunately, a pair would cost about the same as your first car, but if you win the lottery, buy a bundle; you will go faster without a doubt!

Clement has also entered the fat-tubular market with a Griffo largo; the same tire as the original classic Griffo, but in a 30mm width instead of 26mm. These are based on the same casing as the famous Clement criterium road tire — very straight and fast, but still susceptible to sharp rocks or icy rutted ground.

Generally speaking, go for 28mm or 30mm tires front and rear for fast circuits on a hard surface; 30-32mm if it is dry but bumpy; 32mm if it is muddy; and 28mm front and 32mm rear if it is very muddy. This is all based on a Griffo-style tread pattern; change this only for very sandy circuits such as Koksijde, Belgium (world's 1994), when a file tread is more suitable, in 34mm section.

Sticking on and blowing up tires is almost as important as the type of tire you use, as is the pressure at which you run them. The majority of 'cross racers inflate their tires too hard, failing to consider the course surface when inflating them. But using tires at lower pressures requires that they be properly glued on. Otherwise, you are liable to lose them ... always at the point farthest from the pit area!

If you are going to use a tub tape (double-sided sticky tape, favored by road and track riders), use it in conjunction with glue, never on its own, as it is too susceptible to drying out after washing or wet races. It is true that glue takes time and is messy, and with tape you can have a tire on in two minutes. But glue is worth the hassle in the long run. There are very few mechanical problems during a race which make riding to a pit (and a spare bike) an impossible task, but a broken chain and a rolled tire are two that will stop you dead! So spare no effort in your gluing.

The secret to stickiness is the type of glue and the amount. Use a reputable brand — the best are Continental, Vittoria, Clement or Wolber — and a clear glue will not be so obvious if it should leak out a little. Do not be fooled into thinking that more glue equals more stick, as all that will happen is that you will get it all over your rims, hands and carpet.

On a new rim, put on a layer of glue and leave it to dry for a couple of hours. After this initial layer, add a tub tape. Then inflate the tire a little to turn it inside out, and give it two coats. Put another layer of glue on top of the tub tape; leave it for an hour; then fit the tubular. It will never come off, and will probably require tools to remove it when it is punctured or worn out!

If you do not have easy access to tub tape, and use glue only, then follow the directions as above without the tape and you will be fine. Just check your tires more often to make sure they are still stuck!

When you are confident that your tires are glued on securely, you can start racing with them at the correct pressure without fear of rolling them. Your weight and riding style will affect the pressure, as will the course, but experience will tell you what you can get away with. A softer tire will improve traction considerably, but 3-3.5 bars (40-45psi) is as soft as you will go. And certainly no more than 4.5 bars (65psi) will ever be required. Get a track (stand) pump with a reliable gauge and stick by it. Remember that a Clement Griffo with 4 (58psi) bars in will feel softer to the squeeze than a Barum at the same pressure because of their different casings, but do not be tempted to pump the Griffo any harder.

Tires should be checked meticulously every time the bike is cleaned, both for cuts and to ensure they are still stuck on. If you find one needs re-sticking, take the tire off the rim and dry both overnight before re-applying a layer of glue to both rim and tire and replacing.

Gearing

In the old days, it was common to see 'crossers using a single 42-tooth chain ring with chain guards on either side, with a six-speed cluster ranging from 13-26; the more adventurous rider used a double chainset. The fact that you could race with just six gears said a lot about race circuits at that time!

Nowadays, you are not going to get far without a double-chainring set-up, and with the development of cassette hubs, it is harder to avoid using narrow seven- or eight-speed clusters. This is unfortunate, because the old "standard" width six-speed clusters were less vulnerable to clogging. Today's narrower cog spacing means more frequent bike changes to get the offending parts cleaned.

Chain guards were used to keep chains from bouncing off on rough ground, but with the current quality of derailleur springs, a correct chain length and a well-adjusted front derailleur, this should never be a problem.

The size of gearing depends on the rider's ability and the circuit, but as a general guide, 39/48 on the chainset and 13-15-17-19-21-23-26 on the back will suit most people. Juveniles and relative novices would be well advised to change the bottom two sprockets for a 24 and a 28, and perhaps the 48 for a 46 at the front. But you should avoid sprockets larger than 28 at the back for two reasons. The main reason is mechanical; no standard rear derailleur will accommodate a 30 or 32 sprocket, which requires a longer-armed mechanism that is more susceptible to damage from stray sticks and rocks. Secondly, if you are traveling slow enough to need 39x32 during a race, you will be better off running!

Try to use commonly available chainsets and clusters to ease the search for spare sizes of rings/sprockets; this will almost certainly mean either Shimano or Campagnolo. And remember to check compatibility before you start mixing and matching parts, as transmissions always work best when the same manufacturer is used all the way down the line.

This neat little gizmo is called a "Cog Hog" and eases the cable run into the rear derailleur, making gear shifting really smooth and friction-free.

All modern derailleurs designed for road or mountain-bike racing are suitable for 'cross, and all can accept a 39/48 x 12-26 gear set-up. Cheaper derailleurs work just as well as the more expensive models when they are new — they simply wear out quicker. So remember, paying more won't necessarily get you better shifting ... but it may give you more of it.

Shift levers always used to go in the ends of the handlebars, and still do, unless you have ever used STI or Ergopower levers on your road bike ... in which case you will never use bar-ends again! They could have been invented with 'cross in mind, these shift levers incorporated into brake levers. Shimano did it first with the STI lever, Campagnolo followed quickly with the Ergopower lever, and for me, the Ergo is the better choice for 'cross.

Firstly, the cables are all under the handlebar tape, which is neater and doesn't interfere with some bike-carrying styles. Secondly, the way

STI works — with the whole lever moving to change gear — the mechanism can fill with mud or sand, or be damaged more easily, as a result of falls or simply dropping the bike in the pits. Thirdly, the Ergo lever can change down eight sprockets in two moves, whereas the STI needs more clicks and more time.

Both types of levers are indexed to work with their relative sprockets, so as with derailleurs, try to use Shimano with Shimano, and Campy with Campy, when it comes to choosing levers, derailleurs and sprockets.

Bar-end shifters are by no means destined for the 'cross equipment museum; they are now available from the above named manufacturers in indexed form, are significantly lighter than STI-style levers, and are clean, simple and easy to use.

While we're on the subject of gears, don't overlook the cables, as these can affect shifting enormously. Gore-Tex cables are very smooth and stay that way significantly longer than a regular cables; though expensive, they are a worthwhile investment. Take time out to make sure that the outer cable is in good shape, with well-fitting ferrules, and that there are no splits or kinks that will affect the inner cable run.

As for old-style, down-tube shift levers, don't even consider using them ... unless you are going to a '70s-retro race dressed as Roger De Vlaeminck!

Finally, Grip Shift can be used with success, either in the center of the bars, or on the drops. These shifters are light and simple, and have started showing up on a number of 'cross bikes recently.

Pedals

You will notice in the sections on training and technique just how much emphasis is put on the ability to get your feet back in the pedals after remounting the bike. This is a whole lot easier if the pedal and shoe setup is a good one.

Remember toeclips and straps? Remember how they always bent; how you could spend an eternity trying to flick your foot in as your opponents were riding away from you; and how in wet races your toe straps got soggy and always got in the way of a fast re-entry? Obviously, the designers at Shimano remembered those things, too, prompt-

First man on a 'cross bike with clipless pedals, first with two sets of brake levers — the 1995 world champ, Dieter Runkel.

ing them to develop the step-in pedals now universally known as SPDs (Shimano Pedal Design).

Since the introduction of SPDs and the various makes that followed them onto the market, clips and straps are definitely items you can put in the 'cross museum.

In an earlier version of this book, I commented on the early days of step-in pedals. Swiss riders were the first to notice the advantages that these pedal systems could offer the 'cross rider. The Look road pedals first used by Swiss riders offered a variety of advantages for 'cross racers, their coaches said: better use of hip and knee muscles; the ability to "bunny-hop" obstacles with greater security; more safety on descents, as the feet are secure; and more efficient pedaling on bumpy ground, as the foot cannot bounce out of the pedal. These advantages all still hold true with SPDs, but with the added advantage of a smaller cleat that does not interfere with running, as did the old Swiss Look cleat.

The disadvantages of SPDs are few, however, they clog quite easily, although the current PD-M747 clears well. The problems come when you are forced to run on sandy, sticky ground, which clogs the mechanism and causes problems releasing the foot. Like eight-speed clusters, the advantages aren't great, as long as you can get your bikes cleaned well and frequently during races.

The ease with which you can get into the pedals after remounting depends to a great extent on the type of shoe you use, and how much time you give to practicing this skill. See the section on shoes for the best types to go for. Otherwise, if you are still having trouble getting your feet in, don't blame the pedals!

Although Shimano leads the field with the SPD, there are many other types of pedals on the market, all based on the same principles, being double sided, with the shoe held in by a small cleat. Beware of some of the cheaper makes out there; they don't have sufficient spring tension to hold the foot in for strenuous effort, such as the start, and are really designed for the leisure rider. Other than that, if you decide to choose an alternative to Shimano, look for something that will not clog too easily, that is light, and that uses a cleat that will fasten to your chosen shoe.

Brakes

If you are serious about your 'cross, you will certainly have a frame with brazed-on pivots for cantilever brakes. No other brake will do. The main advantage of this style of brake is that it does not clog up with mud. This is also the most powerful brake on the market — something you will be very glad of on a descent — and light and simple as well.

The advent of mountain bikes has introduced a larger number of brake styles and makes onto the market. Some are suitable, but others are not, as they are designed to work with a specific lever only available for use on straight handlebars.

The original and best cantilever brake for 'cross is the Weinmann 420, but unfortunately these have become a rarity as production has ceased. But something based on the same simple design is what you should look for. The closest at the moment is the Ritchey, used by 'cross superstar Thomas Frischknecht plus a gaggle of other riders, or some of the cheaper models by Shimano and their copiers.

The up-market mountain-bike cantilevers, such as Shimano's V-Brake, are rarely suitable as they are designed for use with a cammed lever, only available in a straight-bar design. Most drop-bar brake levers simply do not give enough leverage to work with such cantilevers, and you have to adjust the brake blocks very close to the rim ... otherwise you may find yourself pulling the lever all the way back to the bars without slowing down!

When replacing brake pads, as you invariably will have to, take a look at what is available, especially if you have fitted an economy model brake, as an upgrade on the pads will increase your stopping power.

If you have decided to go with STI or Ergo shifters, then the choice of brake levers has been made for you. If you are sticking to bar-end shifters, then you need to decide on a lever, which is simply a matter of personal choice and hand size. Don't use something that is obviously too big for your hand, either in the reach from the bars, or the size of the lever hoods.

One interesting recent development is the use of an additional set of brake levers on the tops of the bars. This lets a rider brake from a riding position on the tops, as if he were riding a mountain bike. Sim-

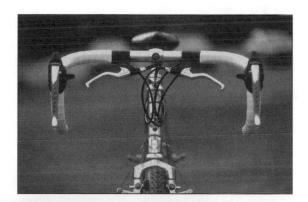

View from the
front of twin
levers and
neat cables.

If you decide to run with
two sets of brake levers,
you will have a lot of
cables to deal with! Keep
them as short as possible,
and use extra cable clips
on the top tube to route
the rear brake cable into
the cable stop on the seat
post clamp bolt.

To get two cables into one
brake hanger, use the purpose built cable stop on the
frame, and add a second
on the clamp bolt.

ply fit a pair of mountain-bike levers to the tops, close to the stem, with an additional set of cables going into the same cable hanger as those from the original levers. It adds weight, but if you ride a lot with your hands on the tops, then it could be for you. This idea comes from the same Swiss guy who came up with the use of Look pedals ... Dieter Runkel. It's obvious what he thinks about when he is out training!

As with gear cables, think about an upgrade on the brake-cable system you use. Gore-Tex also makes brake cables with the same advantages as its gear cables — long, smooth life and a lighter action — and there are numerous other Teflon-coated cable sets around that are worth investigating.

Handlebars, stem and saddle

Bars come in a variety of widths and styles, and the chances are that you already have a favorite model. If so, stick with it. If not, the best shape for 'cross is the square, shallow design similar to the Cinelli 64. The flat top of the bars allows you to ride on the tops with hands relatively wide apart for better control, which a curved bar such as the Cinelli 65 tends to inhibit. Also, the shallow drop does not give such a drastic change of position as the deeper Cinelli 66.

Since the advent of STI-style shifters, these bars are now available with grooves to take the cables under the tape without making an uncomfortable lump. Also popular on road bikes are the more "anatomically" shaped bars such as Cinelli Eubios, which have a shaped drop section that fits the hand shape more comfortably.

All these bar types and styles are available from a variety of manufacturers; if you cannot find Cinelli, look for 3T or ITM, both of which have bars in similar styles.

If you continue to use bar-end shifters and don't like the feel of two sets of cables running under the tape, then put the gear cables inside the bars. Drill a hole about 6-7cm from the end of the bars so that the cable does not go in at too tight an angle, and another hole about 2cm from the stem on the reinforced section in the middle of the bars. Never drill holes on the unstrengthened section on the top of the bars, as this is where breaks occur. If you are in any doubt at all about where to drill or how, consult your local specialist bike shop. Better safe than sorry!

The handlebar stem should always be either the same make as the bars, or at least the same diameter to give a perfect, non creaking fit. Weight freaks can save precious grams on the stem, but usually at quite an expense, as new materials have been recently introduced into stem manufacture.

Saddle technology has gone through the roof in the past few years. New designs, new materials to bring the weight right down, new colors and even saddles with your team name embroidered on!

Weight and comfort are the critical factors here, along with a covering that is going to be easy to take care of and will not hold water. Rails of aluminum and titanium are great for saving weight. But with the constant jumping on, some of the cheaper models just bend too easily, and a bent saddle can cause major bio-mechanical problems if you continue to ride on it. Titanium is strong and light, and San Marco, Selle Royal and Selle Italia make huge ranges of saddles in all sorts of shapes and sizes to suit. Don't forget you are not going to be sitting down for hours on end like a road rider, so you can sacrifice a little bit of comfort if it is going to save you some weight.

Position on a 'cross bike

Let us presuppose that you have your position sorted out on your road bike, and that any changes on your 'cross bike will be relative to this.

Ideally, you should use a position about 1cm shorter in reach, and either the same, or no more than 1cm lower, in saddle height. The best way to achieve this is to use a frame smaller by these measurements. You'll be able to use the same length stem and have the same amount of seatpost showing as on your road bike, and the slightly smaller frame will be better for your bike handling.

Position your brake levers and bars slightly higher, and set your saddle slightly farther back to give yourself a more upright position over the rear wheel and help traction in slippery conditions.

Another tip is to use slightly longer cranks than on your road bike. As with a mountain bike, which invariably come with 175mm cranks as standard, you are effectively pedaling slower on a relatively big gear, and the extra leverage provided by longer cranks can be a real help. If you regularly ride a mountain bike with 175mm cranks, but a road bike with 172.5mm cranks, then go for 175mm on your 'cross bike. If you are small, or use 170mm on the road, use 172.5mm on your 'cross bike. Anything longer than 175mm will create problems with ground clearance.

Saving weight

Saving weight has become the Holy Grail of off-road riders; mountain bikes now weigh less than road bikes did just a few years ago, and the advantages of low weight, especially for a 'cross bike that you have to pick up and carry up hill are obvious.

Saving weight on a bike is a bit like buying a better stereo system. You have to pay twice as much to get a slight improvement in the sound quality. Likewise, you could cut a bike's weight to 18 pounds with relatively ease, but to knock another pound off, you are going to have to spend a lot of time and money.

No doubt about it: mountain-bike technology now means that you can find an alternative to every component on your 'cross bike in something lighter, from rims and tires, to chainring bolts and handlebar tape, but all at a price. If price is a minor consideration (lucky you!), then replace regular bolts with titanium, buy Ti-rail saddles and handlebar stems, replace pedal spindles and seatpost clamps, buy the lightest tires and composite wheels. Just remember that although titanium is lighter and stronger than virtually every other material, you still need a reliable bike that isn't going to let you down during a race. So check out each part you buy, and make sure you think it is going to be reliable.

Care of equipment

Any good-quality racing bike is an expensive piece of equipment; if looked after correctly, it will not let you down during a race, and will last (it is hoped) for a few seasons.

This is even more true for a cyclo-cross bike. Out in all weather, continually being battered by the terrain, and constantly being washed, its life compared to its road-racing cousin will be a short one. So it is even more important to make sure it is 100 percent at all times.

Try to keep one bike purely for racing, and one for training, for your pre-race warm-up, and as a spare during races. It is your spare/training bike that is going to get the most use, but because it is being used frequently, it is easy to forget about it.

Try to put aside some time each week to prepare your equipment. Probably the best day is Friday, which is a light training day, and means you have Saturday to get to the bike shop, should you need to. Do not wait until Saturday night to discover you have a broken wheel spindle when you are supposed to be leaving for a race at 9 a.m. the next day!

Your preparation for the next race starts as soon as the last one finishes. While you are getting changed, your helper should clean both bikes as well as possible and load up the car. When you get home, give the bikes a quick squirt of oil on the chains and put them to bed — and do the same yourself! Do not feel obliged to spend another hour in the yard with a bucket; you will be tired after a hard race, so look after yourself first and save the bikes until Monday, when they should be cleaned thoroughly, dried, oiled and given a quick once-over before going away until Friday's more intensive check.

Cleaning a 'cross bike

Because of the conditions cyclo-cross bikes are subjected to, it is important that they are kept clean; this will prolong the life of the components, and make any maintenance a lot easier and more pleasant.

You should try to get into the habit of washing your bike after every training ride, and as soon as possible after a race. If you get into a routine, it will not take long.

If the bike is especially muddy, use a pressure washer or hose to get rid of most of the mud, then put it on a bike stand to clean it properly. With all the water your bike will be subjected to, especially if you use a pressure washer, you must keep an eye on the main bearings and regrease them regularly, otherwise they will not last two minutes. Try to avoid directing the blast from a pressure washer straight at a bearing, such as the bottom bracket or sides of the hubs. Try to clean these parts from above, where the water cannot be forced into the moving parts quite so easily. Start cleaning with a pressure washer from the top of the bike and work down, then get the buckets out.

For cleaning the bike you will need: two buckets of water, preferably hot, one soapy, one not; a stiff dustpan brush; a sponge; and degreaser in either a sprayer or a container with a brush. There are plenty of citrus-based, water-soluble degreasers available, and they are clean and easy to use. Again, try not to directly spray degreaser into hubs or the bottom bracket when you are cleaning the chainrings and sprockets; direct the squirt from above.

With the bike on a stand, degrease the chain, sprockets and chainrings, then drop the wheels out. Keep the chain under tension with a "sleeping hub" that fits in the dropout. Scrub the wheels and tires with the stiff brush to remove all the mud, then rinse off the wheels and sprockets with clean water.

Moving onto the bike, start at the top and working downward, using the hot water and sponge. If the mud has dried, you will probably need the stiff brush, especially around the brakes and pedals, to loosen the mud before cleaning them properly with the sponge. Do not forget to clean under the saddle with the brush; you will be amazed how much mud ends up under there.

By the time you get to the transmission the degreaser will have worked its magic and loosened up the oil, most of which will have been washed off by the water you've splashed onto the frame. Fill the sponge with water and run the chain through it while turning the pedals, then rinse the chainrings and derailleurs.

Wash the soap off with clean water, and the bike is ready to be dried and checked over.

Checking the bike

If you are methodical, this will not take long, and you are less likely to miss anything.

Look for anything that is worn or stiff and replace it immediately. The transmission is in for a hard time, so chains should be changed regularly — certainly no less than three times a season, and more if a heavy race schedule or a run of bad weather makes the replacement necessary.

Gear jockey wheels also do not last long under wet, gritty conditions, and if they are worn, they make gear changes less positive. You will certainly need to replace brake pads and all cables from time to time, and it is worth considering a major overhaul around Christmastime so that your bike is in top condition for the big races in January and February.

Clothing

The clothing requirements for a 'cross racer do not differ greatly from those of a road racer, but as all your training and racing takes place during the coldest, wettest months of the year, good-quality cycling clothes can make all the difference between a productive training session and a miserable, wet ride where the object is simply to get home.

For racing, the clothing must be well-fitting and comfortable, and suitable for any extremes of climate.

Footwear

Starting at the bottom and working up, undoubtedly the most important item of clothing is the footwear. Yet again, we have the mountain bike to thank for the current large range of shoes designed for off-road riding, but the requirements for a good cyclo-cross shoe are not necessarily the same as those of a good mountain bike shoe, so be on your guard.

Most mountain bike shoes are too stiff to be ideal for 'cross, where the sections covered on foot mean that a stiff shoe will be uncomfortable and too slippery. Try to find a shoe with the following: a slightly more flexible sole at the front to help with the running; screw-in studs or spikes at the very front of the sole; and a fastening system that will not be affected by mud and running. A lot of very good shoes seem to have been designed in areas where it doesn't rain! Ninety percent of the shoe is perfect, but it fastens with a Velcro strap that works fine in the dry, but comes undone as soon as it becomes wet. Some of the ingenious fastenings used by companies such as Sidi and Gaerne are great; very secure, and can even be tightened or loosened during a ride.

The sole should accept the cleat for the style of pedal you have chosen, have an aggressive tread for slippery conditions, and offer removable studs or spikes in the toe and heel for extremes of running up or down hills.

A Shimano shoe clipped into a 747 clipless pedal; note the screw-in studs in the front of the shoe, replaceable for different conditions.

If two bikes are a good idea, two pair of shoes are a better one. Use one pair to train and warm up in, and then a nice clean, dry pair to race in. In this way, last year's racing shoes become this year's training shoes, and so on.

Socks should be cotton or cotton mix, preferably not the cushion-soled sport socks that hold water, and be short and well-fitting. Don't forget to have racing socks on when you try on shoes — a good-fitting shoe is essential if it is not going to be left in a muddy stream!

Shorts

Shorts should either be part of a skinsuit or of the bib variety. Lycra is the norm, but as this comes in a variety of qualities which affect the fit, choose carefully. Also look for synthetic chamois inserts, which can be machine washed easily, and dry quickly.

Shorts are your most important point of contact with your bike; they must fit perfectly and always be clean. Any slight problem will manifest itself as a saddle sore, which invariably means time off the bike to treat, so do not skimp on this purchase!

Jerseys

Skinsuits are now the most popular form of race clothing, in either long or short sleeves, depending on the temperature. They provide a good fit and don't become baggy when wet. During the early season, you can probably get away with wearing a vest under your skinsuit. This should be one of the current style of base-layer garments that wick perspiration from your skin to the outer surface where it can evaporate quickly, leaving you feeling dry and warm. To do this, the under-vest must be close fitting and stretchy; the best base layers are made by Karrimor, Lifa and Sub Zero.

As the winter becomes colder you will need more under the skinsuit, but as the Lycra fabric is stretchy, that should not be a problem. Keep the under-vest as the base layer and add a mid-layer to trap body heat and keep you insulated from the cold. This mid-layer can be either a racing jersey or a very thin fleece layer. Remember that most of these types of garments are not windproof, so if the wind is biting, make sure you have something on that will give you some protection, even if it is just a plastic bag under your skinsuit!

If the temperature drops below freezing, or you are racing in snow, always wear Lycra tights or leg warmers on top of embrocation. And definitely wear some chest protection, either a vest made for the purpose or a do-it-yourself version made out of bubble wrap.

Gloves

Something should always be worn on the hands, no matter what the weather, either fingerless or full-fingered gloves. There are plenty of thermal gloves on the market, but many are too slippery on the handlebars, or ineffective when they get wet. Ski gloves are very warm and usually have some degree of water resistance, but they tend to be bulky, which can be awkward for braking and gear shifting. Gloves made out of Gore-Tex or similar material are by far the best, although thin neoprene material is also very effective in cold, wet conditions.

Gore-Tex is a material containing millions of tiny pores, which allow perspiration to pass out away from the body but do not allow rain in, thus providing a 100-percent waterproof garment without the usual problems of sweating and chilling encountered with other waterproof materials. The main problem is the price ... but if you can afford Gore-Tex gloves, they will be worth the investment.

Other qualities to look out for are a non-slip grip on the palm, and a long wrist to fill the gap between glove and jersey. Wear your watch or heart-rate monitor over the top of your jersey sleeve so that you can see at a glance how long you have been riding without having to move your sleeve up.

Headgear and eyewear

Helmets are obligatory in races worldwide, and since you have to wear one, it may as well be a good one! In most countries, hard-shell helmets are required, although for UCI-sanctioned international races, including the world championships, the old "hairnet" type of helmet is still permissible.

A tremendous amount of heat is lost through the head on cold days, so wear a cotton cap under the helmet. Also, on wet days, have the peak at the front down to help keep water out of your eyes.

Use eyewear if the conditions are exceptionally cold, wet or very bright. As well as protecting your eyes from cold and wet, some lenses can brighten up the dull or flat light common to a wooded area. If the ground is wet and muddy, chances are your glasses are not going to stay clean much past the first lap. But even if you simply wear them for the initial starting effort where water in your eyes is going to be an inconvenience, then throw them off, it will be worth the effort.

In mountain bike races, eyewear changes are regularly done in the feed or "pit" areas; however, to successfully change a bike and glasses each lap is not really going to be practical. Wear them as long as they are effective, then get rid of them!

Warm-up gear

Warming up before a race means just that — getting your body warm — so dress accordingly. And it's better to wear too much than not enough.

Use your spare shoes, warm training tights and tops and rain jacket if required for your pre-race course check, plus your helmet and spare gloves.

Before the start, once you have changed into your race clothes, put back on your extra tops and tights, if you can get them off easily without removing your shoes. These can be discarded at the start line to avoid too much cooling off.

One very useful addition to your bag is a pair of "tear off" leg warmers with either a full-length zip or Velcro, which can be left on until the last minutes before the start, then removed easily and quickly. You will not be able to buy these, so find someone with a sewing machine to butcher a pair for you!

Training gear

Your training gear will be very similar to the clothing you train in all year. But remember, you will be out in all weathers and temperatures, and bad weather — fog and ice excepted — is no reason to miss a training session.

In extremes of cold and wet, wearing a number of thin layers will keep you warmer than just one or two thick items — and as long as you are warm, getting wet is not a problem. Pay special attention to the extremities — head, hands and feet. Good overshoes, gloves and hat will reduce heat loss dramatically. And good-quality base layers, as mentioned earlier, plus long johns in the same material; good-quality tights and jerseys; thermal suits; and rain jackets in modern fabrics; should see you through all but the harshest winter weather.

If you train in the evenings, make sure you are visible to traffic by wearing light-colored clothing for the last layer or some sort of reflective outerwear. Also be sure that your bike has a good lighting system and reflectors, plus mudguards to keep water off your back and legs.

Eyewear is a good idea for training. Use clear or yellow lenses, which will brighten up dull light conditions and keep water, snow and grit out of your eyes. They also help keep your face warmer if the wind is particularly biting.

Also, do not limit your use of embrocation to race days. If you are susceptible to aches and pains in cold conditions, use some heat-generating cream on your legs and lower back, and use Olba throat lozenges or something similar to help you breathe.

Running gear

The last set of training gear you will need to think about is for running in. You will see from the section on training, that running plays a part in your schedule, so do not treat it as an afterthought.

You will not have to wear half as much clothing for running as you do on the bike. Your body generates more heat while running, and there is a lower wind-chill factor, since you are not traveling as fast. Having said that, you will also sweat a lot more, so the first layer should always be one of the base-layer under-vests we have already discussed to wick away moisture. On top of this, cycling tops or sweatshirts are fine as long as they are not too restrictive.

Breathable running suits made out of Gore-Tex or something similar are ideal if you run a lot. They are totally weatherproof, but unlike a standard rainsuit, they do not leave you feeling as though you have been training in the sauna. They are designed for running, and as such the cut means they will not be ideal for doubling up as a cycling garment. But they will make the majority of winter runs a whole lot more enjoyable, and give you no excuse for any missed training sessions!

The most crucial item for spending time and money on is shoes. Just as you would not dream of buying cycling equipment from your local car accessory shop, do not buy running shoes from your local supermarket. Find a shop that specializes in running shoes, and whose staff are runners, even if it is just for your first pair to get the correct model and size. Explain how far you are running and on what types of surfaces, and spend time trying on different makes and models.

The majority of your running will probably be on grass, so go for a suitable cross-country style shoe. This will give you the required grip and support to cope with the stress of off-road running. This type of shoe will not be suitable for running on roads, as the sole will be too slippery and there will not be enough cushioning. If you run on the road, go for a road training shoe, and this is where you need the specialists' advice — the running-shoe market is massive, catering to a vast range of fitness, ability, physique and type of race or training. It may even be worse than buying your first bike!

Embrocation

Almost as important as the clothing you wear to race in, and certainly as important in your battle to keep warm, is the embrocation you use.

Much depends on the weather. As a general rule, creams such as Musclor, Radian or Portia, or light oils such as Sixtus, should be used if it is cold but dry. But these will not be effective in the wet. If it is wet, either cover them with an oil or liquid paraffin, or use a petroleum-based embrocation such as Cramer or Sports Balm, which will not wash off.

Do not limit their use to your legs; if it is very wet and cold, use a warm cream on your lower back, arms, feet and hands. The warmer you start the race, the more chance you have of staying comfortable throughout. And cold feet and hands can be miserable, diverting attention from the job in hand.

Remember that embrocations designed to stay on in wet weather will not wash off in the shower, so use a flannel and a spirit-based sports wash or cologne to remove it. You will know you have not gotten it all off if your legs are still burning in bed! Lemon juice is also very effective if rubbed over the area.

You should also ensure that you start the race with a clear head and effective breathing. A few drops of Olbas oil, either on cotton wool up your nose, or on the back of your glove or collar, together with a decongestant rubbed on your chest, will clear the tubes for an explosive starting effort. ■

CHAPTER 3

TECHNIQUES AND TACTICS

Mounting and dismounting.

W atch a fast-moving string of top-class riders, gracefully glid-ing on and off their bikes and jumping obstacles at speed, and it looks easy. Watch riders at the other end of the scale attempting the same maneuvers, and you can see the skill, timing and nerve it takes, and the vital seconds and energy that can be saved by per-forming these skills well.

The switch from cycling to running, and vice versa, may have to be repeated 15 or even 20 times a lap, depending on the nature of the course; multiply this by the 10 laps of an average race, and suddenly you are performing a single skill up to 200 times during a one-hour event! You must therefore, be able to mount and dismount easily and auto-matically every time, even at a stressful point in a race — for instance, when you have just attacked and are trying to gain vital seconds.

The experience of racing over varied courses and conditions is invaluable in assessing which technique to use. But every technique must be learned during training — the race is no place to try out new ideas!

Dismounting

You've ridden plenty of races, and you know how to get off your bike. But just think for a minute: Do you always do it the same way? Chances are you do, but is your technique right for every condition? The correct technique for a dismount at 20 mph to jump a low hurdle with an immediate re-mount is considerably different from that required for a dismount halfway up an unrideable muddy climb. So let's examine each condition you will encounter during a race.

Unrideable climbs

The most common reason for dismounting is a hill that is too steep or slippery to ride. Before you dismount, select the gear you will want when you get back on your bike. If the climb is partly rideable but too slippery, you will already be in bottom gear when you get off.

If the hill is too steep, approach it fast with your hands either on the brake levers or on the tops of the bars. Swing your right leg over the back

of the saddle, grab the top tube two or three inches in front of the seatpost, and jump off, unclipping your left foot and putting as much weight as you can through your right arm onto the top tube.

If you are unsure about unclipping your foot from the pedal at this late stage, make it the first thing you do as you approach the dismount; unclip your foot and simply rest it on top of the pedal without clipping it back in, then continue as above.

Uphill dismount
A: Ride at speed toward the hill and start to dismount before you begin to lose speed.....
B and C: Keep your hands where they were on the approach, swing your leg over and jump off as you do so; do not put your right leg "through" as on a fast dismount.
D: pick up the bike as you start to run.

As your feet hit the ground, start running, flick the bike up onto your shoulder by the top tube, or down tube, depending on your style (see "Running with the bike," Page 57).

Almost-rideable climbs

If the hill is almost rideable, the time to dismount is just before you start to lose momentum. Don't carry on, riding slower and slower, until you finally stop. You must maintain momentum at all times. A moving bike is far easier to pick up than a dead weight, so it is better to get off too soon and keep moving, than too late and risk stopping altogether.

Forget about holding the top tube as you dismount; you will be traveling too slowly for this technique to work. Swing your right leg over the saddle, and as you push down on the left pedal, unclip it and jump off. Chances are that your hands will be firmly gripping the brake levers. Leave them there. Run the first few steps with your hands still on the levers until you get into your stride, then pick the bike up, shoulder it and carry on running.

Never run pushing your bike. If it is mud that forced you off your bike in the first place, it will suck at your tires, making pushing harder and clogging your wheels as you go. Always run with your bike on your shoulder.

Flat-out dismount

This is usually to clear a hurdle or stream quickly, with a fast remount to get straight back into your stride. This maneuver takes the most skill and nerve, and can save or lose you the most time.

On the final lap of the 1985 world championships, Klaus-Peter Thaler managed to extend a tenuous lead of two seconds over Dutchman Adri Van der Poel when he cleared a hurdle at incredible speed before his entrance into the Olympic stadium and final victory. Similarly, Thomas Frischknecht raced clear on the opening lap of the 1991 world's in the Netherlands by using a high-speed dismount. Gaining a gap on the first obstacle of the race, he held it to the end. These are only two examples of how one skill can give you the edge over a less-skillful opponent.

Fast dismount

A: Approach at speed and in good time swing the right leg over the saddle. Keep both hands on the tops.

B: Place your right hand on the top tube, and put your right leg between the bike and your left leg.

C: With all your weight through your right arm, flick your left foot out of the pedal....

D: Land on your right foot and take one step before the obstacle, lifting the bike straight up...

E and F: ...and running over the obstacle

G: Then take one step after the obstacle, set the bike down, and re-mount.

Hurdles played a part in forcing riders to dismount at the 1996 world's in France. They also provided an excellent advertising billboard for the host city!

Your speed on the approach to the hurdle depends on your confidence and nerve! In training, start off slowly, and increase your speed until you feel confident you can approach the hurdle at race speed.

This is how it works. First, forget about shifting gears. Assume that the terrain after the obstacle is similar to the approach; with proper technique, you won't lose enough speed to need a gear shift.

Your hand position should be the one you feel most confident with the levers and the flat section on the tops of the bars are the favorites. Perhaps it is best to reserve the tops until you are 100-percent confident, as in this position last-minute braking is out of the question, and you are committed to jumping off at approach speed. So try the levers first.

Adjust your speed on the approach to give yourself plenty of time to

A downhill dismount for a ditch or log
A: On a downhill approach like this, control your speed with your front brake, from the lever hoods...
B: Or from the tops...
C: Then dismount as normal onto your right foot and cross the ditch. If the distance to the re-mount is short, run with the bike on the ground; if it is of any significant length, shoulder the bike.

swing your right leg over and get in position for the dismount. You won't slow down much, but you don't want to be hurried into making a mistake.

Your right leg will be between the bike and your left leg — you will find it will adopt a position slightly forward of your left leg. Place your right hand on the top tube — again, two or three inches in front of the seatpost — and lean your body back. With your weight on your right arm, unclip your left foot from its pedal and land right foot first on the ground. Lift the bike up with your right hand, while your left hand remains on the bars or brake lever, keeping the wheels straight so that when the bike hits the ground again it is under control. Clear the obstacle, put the bike back on the ground, your right hand back on the bars, and jump on.

Sounds easy, doesn't it?! The tricky bit is taking as few steps as possible before and after the hurdle, because as soon as you are on foot, you are losing speed. The secret is the weight that you are putting through your right arm onto the top tube. The top guys tend to jump off, take one full step, jump the obstacle on the next step, take one full step after the obstacle, and remount on the fourth. You may find that you need six steps, but constant practice should give you the confidence to try it faster.

When dismounting at speed, it is best to leave your left foot clipped in until the last part of the dismount. You can only do this with a high-quality pedal system and cleats in good condition, as they must release every time without fail; the consequences of a pedal that won't release as you approach a solid obstacle at 20 mph are not good!

The alternative is to unclip your left foot first, before you swing your right leg over. You must then position your foot on the pedal in such a way that it will not clip in by mistake, and hope that there are not any big bumps ahead that could make your foot bounce off the pedal. Personally, I prefer to keep my cleats in good shape and unclip at the last minute, but the choice is yours.

Remounting

There are two different circumstances in which you will be remounting the bike: following a running section when the bike is on your shoulder; and following an obstacle when the bike is just lifted up.

After a running section

Hold the bars with your left hand and the top tube with your right, then lift the bike off your shoulder and put it on the ground. Try to avoid dropping it too hard, as it can easily bounce out of control, making you waste time remounting.

When the bike is on the ground, get both hands on the bars in the position best suited to the next section of the circuit: the drops for a descent; the levers for a climb or any section out of the saddle; or the tops for a relatively smooth section. Then jump on, with as few steps as possible.

You should be able to jump into the saddle smoothly, clip into your pedals and accelerate as second nature, but problems can arise while clipping your feet in. If your pedals and shoes are right, then it is simply a question of practice, and this is the most important practice you can do. You should be able to get your feet clipped in first time, every time. No excuses!

Putting the bike down
A: If you prefer to use the down tube
for all picking and carrying, then put
it down the same way.
B: Likewise if you use the top tube.

Jumping on
A: Land on the saddle with the inside of the top of the right thigh.
B: Note the position of the right pedal, which is ideally placed to push down and click the shoe in.

After an obstacle

Following the rapid dismount for a hurdle, it is most important to make sure that the bike is under control before you jump on. This means putting it down straight and getting both hands on the bars securely. This is awkward to do flat-out while trying to take only two steps before remounting, so practice slowly and build up speed, as with dismounting.

Running with the bike

How you run — and more importantly, how you carry your bike — will significantly affect your ability to breathe properly and keep your upper body relaxed.

The two main techniques for carrying the bike both give you a nice upright style, and the choice between the two will be governed by your build. The taller rider will be better suited to the style with the arm around the front of the head tube and the hand grasping the brake lever. The shorter rider may prefer the style with the arm under the down tube, which then rests in the bend of the arm, and the hand on the dropped part of the bar.

A carrying style never found in the textbooks, but good enough for Switzerland's Beat Wabel ... a former world junior champion and senior bronze medalist.

*The wrong way to carry your bike.
Too much weight of the bike forward
due to incorrect hand position pulling
the front of the bike down. This means
you run bent over and cannot look up.*

Avoid any style that pushes the weight of the bike forward and down with the top tube/seat tube resting on your shoulder. This makes you tend to lean forward, which restricts breathing and forces you to lift your head awkwardly to see where you are going.

You should attempt to run as upright as possible on the flat, and lean forward slightly into any hills you have to climb. Avoid excess swinging of your free arm; it should be used for balance, and swinging it faster will not make you move forward any faster! On steep hills, many riders like to push their left thigh with the left hand to give it a bit more power.

Occasionally, you may have to run downhill if the descent is unrideable or is followed by an immediate return up a climb. Lean back slightly into the slope, and use your free arm for balance. It is important to watch where you are putting your feet, especially if the descent is unrideable because of too many rocks or roots, because falls while running can easily cause injury.

Carrying style
A: The correct way to carry a bike. This style is favored by people with long limbs; it automatically pushes the bike back on the shoulder, while the front wheel and bars are kept under control by the hand on the brake lever.
B: For shorter people, this style with the arm under the downtube is best. The arm can also take some of the weight of the bike and keeps it drawn into the body. The hand again controls the movement of the bars and front wheel, this time on the drops.

Unless the running section is particularly long (most are fairly short sections over logs or up hills) the effect should be a fast burst, not a gentle jog. When running uphill, short, fast steps will mean a better grip; if you overstretch, you have more chance of slipping. On the flat, you can stride out.

Decide during your warm-up whether to use studs, spikes or nothing at all in the front of your shoes. Avoid spikes if you have to dismount on concrete or rocks, as they will be too slippery. If in doubt, do a warm-up lap with each in and see which works the best.

Picking up the bike

Depending on your carrying style, there are two possible ways to pick your bike up. The best, as you don't have to bend down to do it, is to pick up using the top tube (try to learn to flick the bike up in one sharp movement). This method is best if you carry the bike with your arm around the head tube. But if you carry it with your arm under the down tube, you are as well off picking it up with the down tube, as it will then be easier to slide your arm under as you start to run.

To put the bike down off your shoulder, hold the bars with your left hand and take it off your shoulder with your right hand on the top tube.

Incidentally, when changing bikes, don't throw your bike from your shoulder onto the ground, as you can easily bend handlebars and STI shifters this way. Take it off as described, and when it is on the ground, let go or give it to someone.

Cornering

Cornering in 'cross is very similar to cornering on roads, but as you may be encountering slippery surfaces, it is important not to turn the bars excessively or lean too much. You must eliminate as much of the corner as possible by approaching along the correct line so as to cross

Picking the bike up ▶
a: picking the bike up by the top tube.
b and c: picking the bike up by the down tube.

the apex of the bend with a line that is as nearly straight as possible. You must be prepared to feel the bike moving under you, especially in mud or snow, but only experience will tell you how much movement is safe, or when you will slide off.

Use your front brake or a combination of both brakes when approaching a corner, but take the corner itself without brakes to keep the bike under control. Change your line accordingly to avoid cornering on roots or rocks or any slippery surface, as the bike will move a lot more. Your outside leg should be straight with a lot of weight going through it, and your inside leg bent with the knee pointing slightly outwards.

During 'cross races you will encounter an enormous variety of conditions, each requiring a slightly different approach. Only by encountering them all will you know how the bike responds and how you can control it. Confidence in your bike-handling ability and correct tire pressures can make all the difference in the world, and if someone else can get around a corner fast, there is no reason why you can't. It is just a question of nerve! You will only know what your limit is when you have fallen off a few times — usually, it is hoped, during training — and 99 percent of the time you will not hurt yourself as you will simply slide.

The worst surface for cornering on is ice; keep the bike in as straight a line as possible, and avoid any sharp movements and unnecessary braking.

Climbing

Most climbing in 'cross is done out of the saddle, with the hands on the brake levers. The drops should never be used for climbing, as you need your upper body to be as straight as possible to assist with breathing — vital on a climb.

The compromise between traction on the climb and speed is the biggest problem a cyclo-cross rider faces. On long, slippery climbs you must ride slightly out of the saddle with your weight as far back as you can, unlike on the road, where you tend to be over the handlebars with relatively straight arms.

Uphill strength is a great asset,
and attacks launched on a
climb invariably get a result.

Hands on the levers for all short, severe climbs, as shown here.

In this position, there is an awful lot of strain on your forearms and shoulders, and it is not unusual for these parts of the body to tire the quickest. And you cannot afford to sway the bike beneath you as you do on the road; the bike must be kept still and in a straight line.

On shorter climbs, whether you make it up — and if you do, how fast you do it — is determined by your approach speed. You need as much speed as you can get as you hit the climb, so that you can coast up it without having to pedal too much. Do not try to approach the climb at normal speed, change to your lowest gear and pedal up it — you will not make it to the top. The lower the gear you use, the less traction you will have, and wheelspin will bring you to a halt. Using big gears and approaching climbs at speed takes a lot of strength, but this is the best attribute a 'cross rider can have.

A lot of the problems with traction come down to having the correct tires at the correct pressure. As mentioned in the equipment section, most people have their tires pumped up too hard, which seriously reduces grip. Let some air out — you will find it helps a lot.

Descending

A good descender needs two attributes: nerve and skill. The skills and techniques can be learned and practiced, but the nerve is built in; either you have it, or you don't.

The biggest mistake a beginner can make when descending is to go too slow. It is actually easier to go faster, as you ride over things at speed that throw you off balance at slower speeds.

There are a number of points to remember while descending. Avoid too much use of the front brake, as it impairs steering. Also, heavy braking with the back usually locks your wheel. This is okay if it is controlled, but you can easily lose control if your wheel is sliding and you have to corner.

Always descend with your hands on the dropped part of your han-

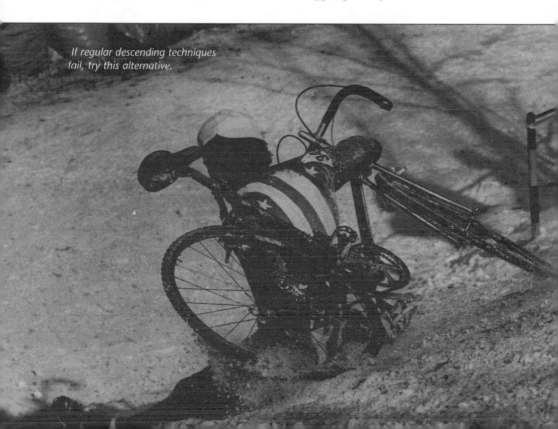

If regular descending techniques fail, try this alternative.

dlebars, as they will be able to reach the brake levers more easily while gripping the bars for security. Ease yourself slightly off the saddle, and keep your weight back, balancing the saddle between your thighs. Let your legs absorb the shocks.

Do not be afraid to unclip a foot on corners or cambers during a descent. If the bike starts to slide, you can dab with your foot and keep yourself upright. If you descend with one foot out, keep the leg that is still in the pedal straight with a lot of weight through it, and use your free leg to balance with. As long as you can clip your foot back in the pedal quickly, you will lose absolutely no time descending with a foot out of the pedal. And the added security can help you avoid crashes while giving you confidence to descend faster than normal.

Sort out your lines down hills during your warm-up. You need to take the straightest line possible, and this may mean descending across the hill to ensure a good line for the next part of the circuit. If you are a confident descender, attacking just before a descent is an excellent way to get a gap. Big time differences can appear between the good and the not-so-good.

Bunny-hopping

Until recently, bunny-hopping an obstacle wasn't really the done thing in a cyclo-cross race. If you came across an obstacle, you dismounted, jumped over it and re-mounted afterward.

Even after Danny De Bie from Belgium won the world championship in France because he could jump the barriers at the bottom of some long run-ups, then ride the run-ups, we didn't see a posse of 'crossmen out practicing bunny-hops on their little brothers' BMX bikes. It was only really when the new breed of mountain bike racers came along that bunny-hopping became fashionable. And once a few started doing it during 'cross races, the rest of the field had to learn pretty damned fast just in order to keep up!

Bunny-hopping, once mastered, can save a lot of seconds on a single obstacle over even the fastest dismounters. And you know by now what that can add up to during a race. Nowadays, no matter how high the obstacle, there will always be someone in the race that clears it aboard his bike, and a whole line of people seeing if they can clear it during warm-up laps.

To bunny-hop obstacles during a race you must be 100-percent confident that you can do it every single time. Nine times out of 10 is no good, because the one time you don't make it will cost you more time than you gained on all the previous nine put together. You also risk doing serious damage to yourself and your bike. If any technique needs rigorous practice during training, this is the one.

There are two types of bunny-hop: the one where you clear the obstacle at speed with both wheels in the air; and the slower, "one wheel at a time" technique used for very high obstacles. The latter is only useful if you can ride a subsequent section of the circuit faster by staying on your bike — say, an rideable climb preceded by an obstacle. Otherwise, it is normally faster to dismount at speed and jump the obstacle.

Let us examine the techniques required for both methods:

A clear bunny-hop

First, make sure your pedals are in good shape, with adequate spring tension to keep your foot in place, as it is by pulling up with hands and feet that you get the bike in the air. Pulling a foot out of its pedal during such a move can have some nasty consequences!

A fast bunny-hop
A: Approach the obstacle at speed, with your hands firmly on the tops. Pull up with the front wheel....
B: The back wheel will follow....
C: And land smoothly on the front wheel with your weight well back.

Your hands may either be on the tops or on the brake levers, but never on the drops, as that messes up your weight distribution. The tops are good for getting lots of pull, but not so good if you need to control your speed at the last moment, unless you have the "extra" set of brake levers (see "Brakes," page 32).

Your position should be fairly upright, out of the saddle with the cranks level, and your weight directly over the pedals. The front wheel should be pulled up first — then shift your weight forward, pull up on the pedals, and your rear wheel will simply follow the front. Do not try to lift both wheels simultaneously. Try to ensure that your take-off is straight and the bike level so that your landing is the same — otherwise, you will be out of control when your wheels touch the ground.

To practice this in training, place something light — a small branch, wooden pole, or curtain rail — on two stacks of bricks. Start low, then gradually add bricks to increase the height. If you hit the bar it will simply fall off, avoiding crashes or damage to wheels.

Riding an obstacle

For riding over an obstacle too high to clear with both wheels, the best place for the hands is on the brake levers. Lift the front wheel up with your weight back; as it lands, throw your weight forward and help the back wheel over by pulling up on the pedals. (See page 67.)

There is a fine line between going fast enough to keep your momentum and get your crankset and back wheel over, and going too fast to get the rear wheel up, with the result that it hits the obstacle too hard and throws you over the bars. Also, if you try to hit the obstacle too slowly, you will find yourself with a wheel on either side of it and unable to move ... probably with a bent chainring or rear wheel as well.

Cambers

If the course is routed across a slope, you will have to contend with the problem of sliding downward when you want to travel straight across. If the camber is severe, you will not be able to pedal, as the uphill pedal will catch on the ground; this means getting as much

A slow bunny-hop
A: On a bigger obstacle it is necessary to approach at a slower speed; lift the front wheel....
B: On, and lift the rear....
C: And land with weight well back again, to avoid a trip over the bars!

speed up as possible before you reach the camber to allow you to free-wheel across the offending section.

Going straight across without succumbing to the tendency to drop down is a matter of weight distribution. As much weight as possible needs to be on the downhill pedal. If the camber is severe, you may also need to shift some body weight over to assist you.

Unless you can get across without any problems, take your uphill foot out of the pedal and leave your leg out; this automatically puts all your weight onto the correct pedal, and if the bike starts to slide you will be able to push yourself back upright quickly before you fall off.

The aim is to stay as high as possible on cambers. If you slip to the bottom, unless the circuit then turns down the hill, you will have big problems getting back up without dismounting.

If you need to dismount on a camber, you will encounter a number of difficulties that require different techniques. If you have to get off on the uphill side, you cannot put your pedal down in its usual place, as it will catch on the ground. So you must jump as the pedal is on its way

Cambers
A: If you can pedal across it, keep your hands on the tops, and eyes firmly on the line you want to take. Don't look down the slope; you will follow the line of your eyes and be forced downwards.
B: If the slope is too steep to pedal on, or it is a downhill camber, hands on the drops, and the uphill leg out to put all the weight over the downhill pedal.

down. If you have to jump off on the downhill side, you will land with your feet a lot lower than the bike, and it will not be easy to get it on your shoulder.

Mud

Just as Eskimos have a hundred different words for snow, so 'cross-men should have a varied vocabulary to describe the different types of mud they encounter. It always differs slightly, and affects the bike and your riding technique in different ways.

Slippery, wet, sticky, clay; mud with grass, with leaves, on rocks, on roots; the list is endless. But all types of mud have the same effect: They slow the bike down. It is amazing just what depths of mud can be ridden through. But a lot of it comes down to momentum, a rider's best friend, and letting the bike go where it wants.

A "light" riding style is needed to get through mud: hands on the tops, using a gear that won't be a struggle should you encounter a particularly bad section, and confidence enough to let the bike make its own line. The right style is neither in the saddle nor standing on the pedals, but halfway between the two, lifting yourself up very slightly off the seat to get more power while maintaining traction.

Again, tire pressure is vital! Soft tires give a much better grip in muddy conditions. The only excuse for hard tires is when the circuit is rocky or has sections through hard, icy ruts that cause compression punctures (pinch-flats). The best tire treads for mud are an arrow design, with maybe a small, square stud pattern on the front wheel.

The biggest problem with mud is that it clogs your bike up. A nice, light 18-pound bike can double in weight in a couple of laps, especially if the mud is mixed in with grass, which grinds gears to a halt and fouls the wheels. Change bikes regularly in muddy races; if you can't change bikes for some reason, then run the really bad bits, and as you are running try to scrape off the worst of the mud. If there are any particularly wet sections on the circuit, riding through these can also help clean wheels and frame.

Sand

Sand is the hallmark of a Dutch 'cross race, and is very awkward stuff to race in. On the bike, it slows you down very quickly indeed, and is impossible to steer a course through. On foot, you feel like you are going nowhere fast, particularly uphill.

On the bike, you should hold the bars firmly on the tops with an upright style, and attempt to hit the sand fast in a big gear and churn your way through it. The bike will make its own mind up which way to go, so you must just hold on and keep pedaling, because as soon as you start to freewheel you will simply stop.

If the section is short and as quick to run, then do it. Sand is a complete wrecker of equipment; 10 laps through a 50-meter stretch is enough to necessitate a new chain and sprockets, together with a total strip-down of the rest of the bike. It gets everywhere, and if not removed, will destroy bearings before you know it.

If you find yourself racing in sand a lot (maybe when you re-locate to the Netherlands) then fit fat tires to your wheels. A minimum of a

Regardless of the severity of the slope, running in sand is always hard work. If you don't like it, avoid 'cross racing in the Netherlands!

32mm tire, either clincher or tubular is required, and 34mm or 36mm are not uncommon. As tread design does not really have any effect in sand; a lot of riders use a file tread front and rear, which is faster on any road sections.

Sandy courses are definitely the places to break out the deep-rim wheels, either tri-spoke design or a deep rim on a spoked wheel. The rim cuts through the sand significantly better than spokes, and provides more steering control.

To run effectively in sand, a style similar to a duck waddling is best. During training before the world's in Koksijde, Belgian coach Eric De Vlaeminck told his riders to put their feet in the footprints of the guy in front; the sand is already compressed, and requires less effort to run.

Ice

Ice is very hard stuff to race on. Riders from countries where there is a lot of ice and snow during the 'cross season, such as Switzerland and the Czech Republic, have a great advantage over riders from countries with more temperate climates, who rarely encounter it for more than a couple of races each year.

Lack of confidence is the biggest problem to overcome on ice. As soon as you start to get nervous, it becomes very hard to stay upright. You must stay on top of it all the time and be positive. A big advantage on an icy circuit is a low center of gravity, as is the ability to roll a big gear with very little upper-body movement.

Racing on ice and snow is a tricky business. Consideration has to be taken as to which tires to use, how hard to run them, what to wear and which lines to take. Sometimes, as shown here, you have to go sideways to go forwards!

A file-tread tire at the front is a must, and something with a small tread at the back — definitely no big studs, either on front or rear. Also, fat tires — 30-32mm — are an advantage. Pressure should be as little as you dare use, unless any of the circuit is sharply rutted, in which case you may need a little bit more to avoid pinch-flats.

Braking on ice causes big problems, too. Never brake hard or suddenly — always use gradual braking, and try to avoid locking up your rear wheel, as it will simply slide away from you.

Shoe grip for running on ice is awkward to achieve. Studs simply slide, so try spikes, which will get more grip on hard ice. And remove any heel studs if there are any downhill runs.

Snow

Snow is totally different from ice. Resembling mud if it is deep, snow is not as slippery to ride on, and you can afford to use a rear tire with more grip ... but keep a file tread on the front, which will steer better.

The biggest problem with snow is braking in it, as it coats both rims and brake pads. This means braking has little effect until the snow has worn off, so extra care must be taken on descents.

Bear in mind that when snow becomes compacted after a number of laps, it takes on all the characteristics of ice, so the advice in the section above should be heeded. Alternatively, a snowy circuit on a warm day can become a mud bath by the end as the thaw kicks in while races progress. Keep your eyes open as conditions change, and particularly look out for new lines that develop.

Although your bike will appear clean, you still must change bikes regularly. The sprockets quickly become full of snow, causing the gears to jump, and your chain will require lubing more often.

Rocks and roots

Wherever possible, both should be avoided if an alternative line can be found around them. The main problem with rocks is the punctures they cause, and any course with rocky sections should be ridden with harder tires, around 4 bars (58 psi).

Wooded courses always contain a lot of roots, which become unearthed as the race progresses. They can be very troublesome, as you get absolutely no grip when crossing them. Try to avoid riding your front wheel over them, as this will simply bring you down. Instead, pull your front wheel up and over to clear them, just leaving your rear wheel to follow. This will invariably slide too, so attempt the same lifting maneuver with the rear and try to bunny-hop over it, or at the least unweight it a little.

Tire pressures have relatively little effect on roots, although a harder tire will generally slide more, so consider the rest of the terrain before choosing your tire pressures. ■

CHAPTER 4

THE ROLE
OF THE
MECHANIC

As soon as your cyclo-cross becomes even slightly serious, you will appreciate the need for a spare bike. Indeed, any race on a muddy circuit will leave you at a considerable disadvantage if you try to compete on the same bike for the whole race. As the laps go by, your bike will get heavier and heavier, your wheels will jam up with mud, and your gears will start jumping as the sprockets get clogged with mud, leaves and grass.

Your first spare bike will probably be an old training bike or even a road bike — simply something to do a lap on every so often while somebody cleans your best bike. As you progress, you will end up with two or even three identical bikes and change them every lap, which means you are always on an immaculate bike and your mechanic can get your bikes clean more easily.

This chapter is for the benefit of your helper, mechanic, manager, masseur, coach, adviser and gofer. Whether it's spouse or sweetheart, parent or friend, teammate or professional mechanic, you cannot do without an assistant, so it is important that he or she become involved and learn what is required to help your races run smoothly. As you improve, so will your assistant. ... and if you become a winning team, then you will share equally in the joys of victory.

I first found myself in the pits helping a rider's girlfriend, who was having difficulty getting the bike clean on a relatively short lap. From such humble beginnings I "grew" with the rider, and as he improved his race results, I discovered new routines to make my job easier and more efficient. The result was extensive travel to international races and numerous world championships with professional and national teams. And just as the newer riders watch the stars to pick up riding tips, so I watched the mechanics to the stars, to see how the job should be done.

Riders come and go, team line-ups change, but as a mechanic I have been able to work with the best. The rider whose girlfriend I helped in the early days, David Baker, went on to many successes as a professional rider, culminating in a top-10 finish in the professional world championships; today, he is one of the leading mountain bike racers in the world.

Although I no longer work directly with David, his results are always of special interest to me, as are those of all riders whose bikes I have cleaned. And who knows? Maybe one day it could be you working in a top racer's pit, freezing your hands in the cause of a shiny bike!

Equipment

For life in the pits, the first thing to take care of is your clothing. You are going to get wet and cold, so dress accordingly. Waterproof footwear and trousers are a must, with plenty of warm clothing on top and a waterproof jacket if the weather is bad. Also, wearing your rider's team jersey will help identify your allegiance and make it easy for him or her to pick you out in the crowd.

Gloves are impractical, as your hands will always be in water, but rubber gloves are okay if it is really cold. Personally, when my riders are getting ready and putting on embrocation on their legs, I either rub some of the cream into my hands, or simply do their legs for them. With some of the hotter embrocations on the market, it can almost be a pleasure to put your hands in an icy stream to cool them down!

Footwear needs reasonably good tread; pits can become muddy, slippery places. And you may end up in streams, fetching water or cleaning bikes, so plan accordingly.

The next thing you will need is buckets. I take three — stable, rectangular ones that fit inside each other. The top one carries all the bits I will need during the race, leaving two to fill with water if there is none available near the pit.

In the top bucket, I will have a small bag with tools (a shoe bag or fanny pack is best). It will contain the following items:

- Spare gear and brake cable
- Allen wrenches (3, 4, 5, 6, 8mm)
- Open ended/ring spanners (7, 8, 9, 10mm)
- Campagnolo T-bar spanner
- Headset wrenches
- Crank-bolt wrench (if not Allen key fitting)
- Pliers
- Chain riveter
- Small screwdriver for gear adjustment
- Spoke wrench
- Insulation tape

With so many multi-tools now available, it is almost possible to pack the above into a couple of pocket-size tools; check out your local mountain bike shop.

Also in the bucket will be cleaning and lubing items:

- Sponges, medium size. Hard are best as they do not fall apart on spokes or cable ends
- Brushes. Small, stiff, for scrubbing wheels and SPDs
- Dry cloths, for drying the bike after washing (Old T-shirts are best.)
- Thin screwdriver, or spoke. For cleaning between sprockets when it is really clogged up
- Spray lubricant. Both thick and thin, depending on the course and weather conditions

The last thing you will need is one spare pair of wheels per bike.

Setting up your pit area

Unfortunately, some course designers do not give adequate thought to pits, their size and position. Some even try to make life hard for the riders by positioning pits on sections of the course that are fast and rideable, or where to change bikes would be a disadvantage. It is a shame if a rider loses a race because he is forced to change bikes in a bad pit.

In smaller races, pit areas are not always provided, and you can choose where you want to set up. While the riders are training on the course prior to the race, take a walk around and try to find the best place. The main consideration is to find a point where the rider is already forced to dismount. The second consideration is the availability of water, especially if the circuit is muddy.

If there is enough mud on the circuit to clog up the bike, it is best to change bikes each lap. It is easier to clean a bike after a single lap than to wait two or three laps and let it get really bad. It might not then be possible to get it completely clean within a lap, and if on that lap your rider punctures, he is not going to be able to get a clean spare.

If you decide to change every lap, you will not have enough water in your two buckets for, say, 10 cleans, so you need to find a water source, be it stream, tap, or pond. I have even cleaned a bike in a puddle which was nowhere near the circuit. The race was muddy, and there was no water to be found anywhere. Following each bike change, I would jump on the bike and pedal to my puddle in the middle of nowhere, clean it, and return just in time to change again.

After that race, I had probably ridden the same distance as the rider; at least, it felt that way, what with flat-out riding and cleaning for one hour. But as it took most of the race for the other mechanics to figure out what I was up to, and since I had a clean bike while they were trying to scrape off the worst of the mud with their hands, I could feel a certain sense of achievement!

If there is no water about, or you are tied to a pit with nothing close by, you will have to resort to your buckets, which you can fill somewhere and leave in the pit before the start. You will simply have to be more sparing with what you use!

Bike changing

Bike changing is certainly worth practicing with your rider before the season gets under way, so that both of you understand the different methods of bike changing before finding yourselves in a race situation.

There are two ways to hand a bike up: straight onto the rider's shoulder if the pit is situated partway up or at the bottom of a run-up; or on the ground if the pit is situated on the flat or at the top of a run-up.

Whichever method is used, the rider must first drop the bike he is using. Ideally, he should hand it to someone, but if no spare hands are available, he should drop it to the side of the course where it will not interfere with following riders. Many a rider has slung his bike down in the middle of the course in front of his opponents, only to see them simply run over it, bending wheels as they go!

As cyclo-cross rules state that no part of the circuit may be covered without a bike, the rider must make sure he is only a step or two away from his helper when he drops his bike. All major races have commissaires in charge of the pits, and they are quick to notice riders running without a bike. Once is a verbal warning; twice is disqualification.

If the clean bike is being handed up on the ground, the helper should have it in the correct gear for the following section of the circuit, with the cranks parallel to the ground and the right pedal facing forward. The helper should hold it by the bars and saddle, then let go of the bars as the rider grabs them, and push the bike by the saddle to help the rider keep his momentum.

If the situation dictates a bike on the shoulder, the helper should hold the bike in the air by the seat tube and handlebars, with the bars slightly over to the left if the rider carries the bike with his arm under the down tube (see "Running with the bike," page 57). As the rider runs past the pit, the helper should run a few steps alongside him and place the bike on the rider's shoulder.

It will take some practice for the rider to let the mechanic do this. The rider's natural reaction is to try to take the bike from the helper before it is on his shoulder. If the mechanic lets go with the bike unbalanced, the rider will have to juggle it, upsetting his rhythm, before he can get it on his shoulder correctly.

The perfect bike change; mechanic and rider in perfect harmony.

The main problem with bike changing comes when the pit area is too small or too congested. On early laps before the field has strung out, you can find 50 mechanics all trying to get in a position to first see, then service their riders. In this situation, it is imperative to make sure there is someone to catch the discarded bike, as there simply will be nowhere to put it.

Cooperation between mechanics can make life in the pits a lot easier. Remember that the race is between the riders — there is nothing to gain by an aggressive attitude in the pits. If your rider has already passed, or has not yet arrived, stand back out of the way until he does arrive. Work out who are the helpers of riders closest to yours, and spread out a bit to give yourself some room.

Bike cleaning

Once your rider has successfully changed bikes, you will probably have about six minutes before he re-appears, expecting an immaculately clean bike. Three minutes spent panicking reduces your cleaning time, so keep calm, stick to a routine, and all will be well.

Cleaning technique depends on your water supply. If you can get to a stream shallow enough to stand in with the bike, then there are no problems.

A perfect bike wash — easy access, not too deep, and plenty of it!

Start by spinning the wheels fast in the water; this will clean the tires very effectively. Then with a sponge, start at the top of the bike and work down. Saddle, bars and brake levers and the three main frame tubes can be done in a matter of seconds. I do the rest of the bike from behind, with the rear wheel supported between my knees. Pedals are next, and can be done with a brush if necessary.

Then comes the most important part — the transmission. Spin the pedals backwards, and with your spoke or thin screwdriver clean the sprockets and between the chainrings. Use your fingers to clean the jockey wheels on the gear mechanism. Sponge off the remainder with a lot of water, and the bike should be clean but wet.

Get back to the pit so you can catch up with the state of play in the race, and while waiting for your rider, dry the bike with your dry cloth, especially the saddle, bars and frame tubes. Oil the chain, jockey wheels and front and rear derailleur with your spray lube, and the bike should be ready to hand back.

Any time you have between finishing cleaning and your rider appearing should be spent giving the bike a once-over. Spin the wheels to check they are straight and not catching the brakes; shift through the gears; and check to see that the bars and brake levers have not been knocked askew due to a crash or simply dropping the bike in the pit. When you are satisfied it is all okay, get the bike in the correct gear, with the pedals set up as described above.

If time or water are short, you must do as much as possible to make the bike as efficient as possible. The main areas that clog up are the wheels, pedals, brakes, sprockets and bottom-bracket area.

Start with the wheels. With insufficient water, you are fighting a losing battle trying to scrub them with a brush, so get your big screwdriver, hold it next to the tire sidewall and spin the wheel, scraping the worst off. A pair of fingers seems to work just as well, but is slightly less glamorous!

Use your spoke to clear the sprockets and chainrings, and fingers on the jockey wheels. If the transmission is free of mud and has a spray of oil, it will work fine, so pay attention to this.

Then, poke out mud from the pedals, brakes and bracket, in that

Big-time bike washes. Only at the world's can a mechanic expect to find help at the bike wash. This system, used at the championships in Switzerland, worked like a dream.

order, and then spend time cleaning the bars and brake levers. This may sound strange, but when a rider jumps on his bike, all he will see are his bars and front wheel, and he will feel if the transmission is smooth. The rest of the bike can still be covered in mud, but he will not know. He will think the whole bike is clean, and concentrate on the race, not thinking how bad the bike feels and wishing he could get a decent mechanic!

Pressure washers

Many race organizers nowadays supply them, and many riders have their own. They certainly take the hard work out of bike cleaning.

The smallest, most portable models are electric and need a power supply off mains or a generator. As most pits don't have a ready supply of electricity, you really need to find a gasoline-powered cleaner that is small and light enough to get into a pit. They also use a lot of water, so the supply needs to be plentiful; it also needs to be clean. Do not try to take water straight from a stream through the cleaner, as it will block up with debris within a couple of laps and take a couple more to clean out and re-prime, leaving your rider floundering on a messy bike.

If you are going to go down the pressure-washer route, either do it properly and be certain it is going to start, work and stay unclogged for the duration of the race, or simply give it a miss and stick to the buckets. They are slower for sure, but at least they're reliable!

I have had mixed results with gas-powered cleaners, and prefer to run an electric cleaner off a small generator, which works perfectly. I also use a large trash can for the water supply, and have a large filter over the top of it to keep any stray bits of grass or leaves from finding their way into the machinery.

With a washer, you are going to get wetter yourself than if you are cleaning out of buckets, particularly when you clean the wheels, so be warned! It is also better if you have a bike stand available to keep both hands free for cleaning, and also to ease wheel cleaning.

Start cleaning at the top, as normal, and work down, spraying wheels and sprockets as the wheels spin. Pay attention to pedals. It is still worth having a bucket and sponge on hand to rinse the bits you have missed once the bike is down off the stand. After the bike is clean, proceed as above with the drying and checking.

Other duties

Not only are you a mechanic during the race, but you must fill the role of manager/adviser as well.

Before the race, take a walk around the circuit. Watch any preceding races and other riders warming up. Make mental notes of the lines they are taking, whether certain sections are a ride or a run, and note any areas that might be congested on the early laps. Your rider should do the same. Between you, you should be able to iron out quite a few problems before the race starts.

Once the race is underway, most riders want to know their position, time gaps in front and behind, and the general state of the race — whether they are losing time on the leaders and how much of the race is left. Most riders do not want to hear "you are doing well" or "you are catching them." A clear time check goes down a lot better. After the initial laps have passed and the race has sorted itself out, I try to give two times: the gap to the rider in front (or behind if my rider is leading); and how much time has passed, which is quite important if there is no lap board.

Offer advice if you can see your rider is taking a wrong line or trying to ride something that other people are running faster. He might not take your advice, but it's better to be told than never to know.

The only other thing that you must train your rider to do is communicate clearly any mechanical problems that force him to make a bike change, other than for a simple clean. Punctures are pretty obvious, even to the most un-mechanical person, but a rider throwing his bike down and screaming that it doesn't work is not much help!

During a race in Luxembourg, my rider changed bikes, telling me his gear shifter was loose, which caused the gears to slip all the time. Unfortunately, through his gasping, what he said sounded nothing like that. I guessed he wanted his headset tightened, which is what I did, and gave the bike back to him on the next lap. He jumped on, and within 200 meters all I could hear was the crunching of his gears and his oaths ringing round the woods! Suffice it to say, the next time he changed I got the message, tightening his gear shifter and loosening his headset.

In cyclo-cross, the rider is much more reliant on his helper's support than in any other branch of the sport, and for the helper it is very hard work. Having both ridden and helped as a mechanic, after a particularly muddy race, I am still in two minds about which is the harder! I have certainly ended up just as dirty. But as with other "back-room" jobs, it is good to know you have contributed to a rider's success. ■

CHAPTER 5

RACE ROUTINE

All the efforts put into your training regime — the hours on the bike in all weathers, the running, the weight training, the stretching, the attention to diet, and the early nights while your friends are out partying — have a single aim: the race. Racing is what it is all about; the bottom line. Some races are not taken as seriously as others. Small local races may be used as a means to an end, to help prepare for a major race in the future. But even in these races your race-day routine should be the same as for the big event, so that come the big day everything is just that — a routine.

Having said that, you must still be flexible and not be thrown into a panic if your routine is broken. You may find yourself racing abroad, for instance, where your normal pre-race meal is not available, or where supporting races mean no training on the circuit. But this should not be allowed to upset you.

It is impossible to put down on paper the "ideal" routine. Traveling times vary, as do races' start times, so you must get to know what works best for you. However, there are some basic points that should be noted, so let us take a look at a "normal" race day.

The race day

Preparation for a Sunday race should start on Friday. A relatively light training day, this is the day to sort out your equipment so that any problems can be rectified on Saturday.

This is also the important night for sleep, so get an early night. Saturday may find you in a strange bed, if you have traveled to the race the day before, and this — combined with restlessness as pre-race nerves start to take hold — might mean a good sleep escapes you. If you have had a good night's sleep on Friday, you will be fine on Sunday.

Train on Saturday as normal. The important part of the day is the evening meal. The aim here is to top up the energy levels, so the meal should be high in carbohydrates — ideally pasta, rice, baked potatoes or bread, with perhaps chicken, salad or vegetables. Make sure you leave a few hours between this meal and bedtime, as sleep on a full stomach is not a good idea.

If your main race starts at around 2 p.m., say, with a supporting race at midday, then your breakfast should be at around 8-8.30 a.m., and your pre-race meal no later than 11 a.m. The two meals should be combined if the race start is midday or earlier.

Breakfast should be what you are normally used to taking. Cereals, müesli, toast with honey or jam is fine; light and nutritious. Avoid anything too heavy, and definitely steer clear of fried food, such as bacon and eggs. The pre-race meal should again be something light but high in carbohydrates. A small pasta dish, omelette, or scrambled eggs and toast — something quick, easy, tasty and nutritious is what you are looking for. No need to go overboard and fill yourself with steak, rice and salad; you are racing for one hour, not a six-hour road race!

Certain things you must remember with regard to race-day diet: Do not take large quantities of sugar or confectionery; complex carbs are a lot better. If pre-race nerves or a tight travel schedule mean that you cannot get a meal down, then use sports drinks and snack bars that are high in complex carbs. Drinks based around glucose polymers, and bars such as PowerBar, Clif Bar, High 5 bar, are all ideal. Above all, do not eat anything within two hours of the start.

Before the race

Aim to arrive at the race in good time; a minimum of two hours before is ideal. Don your warming-up clothing and, on your spare bike, start inspecting the circuit. Your helper should also be looking at the circuit, perhaps walking a lap. He will be looking for the pit areas, availability of water, and locating the changing rooms, registration area, and toilets.

Aim to complete three or four laps during your warm-up. Sort out your best lines and which gears to use in which sections, and also any variations on the course you could use. These will come in especially useful if you find yourself with company toward the end of the race, or start lapping the tail-enders, as you can take your "secret" alternative route to make an attack or pass someone without getting held up.

Pay particular attention to any muddy sections of the course that might get worse as the race goes on. Perhaps there is a longer route available that is drier? Your course inspection is the time to find out, not during the race. Your course inspection should also include the start area and first section of the course, which is quite often on a loop not included on the lap. Decide on the fastest line at the start. If the start area is narrow, you will have to position your helper on the line with your bike some time before the start to ensure you get your spot.

Finish your training on the course about an hour before the race starts. Have one last drink if you need one, and then head for the warmth of the changing rooms to change into race clothing and apply your embrocation.

Make sure you do not head back out to the start in just your skinsuit; put on some warm tops and your tear-away leg warmers. Now, on your best (start) bike go for a warm-up on the road. This should be for between 15-20 minutes at a pace where you just start to sweat, or at around 50-60 percent of your maximum heart rate. Do not go into the anaerobic zone, or higher than 80 percent of your max heart rate, as this will produce a lactic acid build-up that will inhibit your starting effort.

You should arrive at the start area in good time, and if you have your helper positioned on the line keeping your spot, then you can spend the final minutes slowly circling, keeping warm, and focusing on the job in hand.

Keep your extra clothing on as long as possible; the object is to keep warm so that you are ready for a violent starting effort.

After the race

When the race finishes, the most important thing is getting back into some warm, dry clothing. If possible, have someone at the finish with a clean jersey and hat, so you are presentable — should you be required for a presentation. If you are not needed, do not hang about having a post-mortem with the guy who finished 36th; instead, go for a five-minute warm-down, then head for the changing rooms and a hot shower!

Preparation for the next race starts as soon as the last one has finished, so make sure you leave the changing rooms feeling nice and warm, with dry hair, and warm clothes and a hat.

The most important concern after a race (or indeed a training session) should be refueling as quickly as possible. Unfortunately, the ability of muscle to replenish its glycogen stores is greatest during the first hour following exercise, when eating is the last thing you feel like doing. Getting some carbs down within an hour of the race will be of great benefit, so resort to the glucose polymer drinks or one of the specific after-race drinks available that are high in carbs and protein, and have a bottle in your bag to drink in the changing rooms.

What to take to a race

Differences in weather over a 'cross season can mean big variations in the amount of clothing you will need on race days. However, you must be prepared for all eventualities, with clothing to suit all conditions.

Listed below are items you should have in your bag at all times. Do not forget a good supply of plastic bags for putting wet, muddy clothing in to keep it separate from dry items.

Warming up kit
- Shoes
- Socks
- Shorts
- Two under-vests: one short-sleeved, one long-sleeved

- Short- and long-sleeved jerseys
- Training tights
- Training jacket
- Thermal jacket
- Waterproof jacket
- Training hat
- Gloves (full and open-fingered)
- Tear-away leg warmers

Race kit (separate from above)

- Helmet
- Shoes
- Socks
- Shorts or skinsuit
- Short- and long-sleeved jersey
- Arm warmers
- Under-vest
- Leg warmers or Lycra training tights
- Gloves (full and open-fingered)
- Cotton and waterproof caps
- Chest protector
- Two towels: one for embrocation, one for after race
- Shower gel and shampoo
- Sports wash and flannels for removing embrocation
- Embrocation box
- Safety pins
- Shoelaces, or spare shoe fastenings
- Bottles with pre- and post-race drinks
- Small first-aid kit
- Racing license
- Plastic bags
- Flask

If you find yourself traveling abroad to race, do not forget your passport. Also, you will find yourself spending large amounts of time sitting in cars and hotel rooms, so to make life a little more bearable, it is useful to take the following as well:

- Travel kettle or heating element
- Box containing tea, coffee, chocolate, powdered milk, sugar, spoon, etc.
- Personal stereo and selection of tapes or CDs
- Books and magazines
- Travel plug for overseas electrical outlets ■

CHAPTER 6

THE RACE

nlike road racing, in which tactics can play a large part in the outcome of the race and the fittest man does not necessarily win, cyclo-cross tends to be a lot more straightforward. Barring accidents, the best man is usually first across the line.

However, this does not mean that tactics cannot be employed. Where a leading group is comprised of riders of a very similar ability, such as in a world-championship event, the rider who uses his head as well as his legs will come out on top.

Case in point: the 1996 world's, where Dutchman Adri Van der Poel found himself clear on the final lap with two Italian riders. Outnumbered, the odds of an Italian victory were high, but Adri is a master tactician, and playing to his strengths he easily won the final sprint.

Modern 'cross at the top level does not see the "horses for courses" riders who were around a few years ago. Sure, all riders have their personal preferences for a circuit or weather condition, and there are always riders around who will excel in one extreme or another — in heavy mud or on ice — but generally, the best riders are all-arounders who can shine on all types of courses.

It is important not to get into a situation where you think that certain conditions do not suit you, as every time you encounter them, you will be psychologically beaten before you start. If you are espe-

It is important on road sections to keep concentrating and keep the effort high.

cially gifted as a runner or prefer to race on ice, then by all means use this to your advantage. But it is important to work on your weaknesses and become an all-around rider rather than a specialist. By riding to your strengths and limiting your losses on your weaknesses — and by knowing your competitors' strengths and weaknesses — you will have far more success than by blindly hammering away from start to finish in the hope that you will win.

Having said that, it is no use working out your race-winning move if you are not near the front of the race to use it!

The start

The start of a cyclo-cross is vital. A good start will give you a psychological advantage, as you can then concentrate on the rest of the race. You will be aware of who is up near the front, have a clear run around the circuit and not lose time fighting your way past slower rivals.

A fast road start is a frantic place to be, and the front is the best position to get yourself into. At international races, it is essential to be in the top 10 before the course narrows down.

A bad start, especially on a circuit with a number of narrow sections that cause bottlenecks, can be disastrous. The usual response to a bad start is panic: You work too hard to get to the front too quickly, try passing riders where the course won't permit it, and make mistakes. You probably crash a few times, and the great job you did getting psyched up before the race start is wasted as you lose concentration and give up the fight.

If you are unlucky enough to have a poor start, it is important to remain calm and concentrate on gradually working your way back up to the front. If you put in a blistering two laps, the chances are high that you will simply blow up, spending the rest of the race trying to recover. It is not the end of the world. And remember this: There may be 20 or 30 riders in front of you, but on early laps, if everyone is still together, you may only be 20 seconds off the lead.

If you have prepared yourself properly before the race, warmed up well, reconnoitered the start area and the first part of the circuit, and are concentrating on the job in hand, then your start should not let you down.

Practice during training should mean that your foot goes in the pedal first time, every time. Start in a gear that is big enough so that your first pedal revolution does not come around so fast that it makes the free pedal spin, but small enough so that you can accelerate fast for the first two or three revs to get some space. When your foot is in and you have got the revs up, shift up, get out of the saddle and go for it!

Be aware of the riders around you — if there are riders in front, look for gaps to go through, and at no time look down or lose concentration. At this time, there is no real need to hit the front, unless there is a narrow section coming up. Sit near the front, ideally among the first five or six riders, so you can keep an eye on what is going on and follow any moves. Try to settle into a rhythm as quickly as possible.

If your start didn't go as planned, and you find yourself farther back in the field, then it is even more crucial to concentrate. If the start is on a road, as most continental races are, then you can forget about moving up until the first sections of 'cross are reached. Save energy ... but if the opportunity comes to move up, if a gap suddenly opens in front of you, make the most of it and make short, sharp efforts to move up. Keep your head up, and be aware of who is around you; if there are some fast wheels around that you can follow, then so much the better.

Race tactics

Presuming your start has been a good one and you find yourself in the leading group, then what tactics can you employ to ensure a victory?

This is where your knowledge of the circuit, of your own strengths and weaknesses and those of your opponents, will come into play.

If you are a strong runner, then you should use the running sections to attack decisively or on early laps to wear down the opposition. If you are capable, running sections are a good place to attack; unlike on the riding sections, it is of no benefit physically for someone to "sit" on you, as the slipstreaming effect while running is negligible.

Another good place to make your move is on any obstacle or part of the circuit that you can ride but for which your rivals must dismount. If you are confident, say, of riding a log that everybody else is running, on early laps you too should run it until the time for your attack, when you will have the element of surprise and the advantage of being on your bike and ready to attack out of the obstacle.

Danny De Bie, the 1989 world champion, used exactly this tactic during the race at Pontchâteau, France. Although confident he could ride the 40cm barriers at the bottom and top of a number of the run-ups, on the early laps he dismounted like the rest of the 12-strong leading group, thus not drawing attention to himself until his time came to attack. Once he had gained his initial gap, he continued to ride the hurdles, gaining five seconds over his chasers on each run-up and finishing over a minute ahead.

Your pre-race course inspection should have included finding any faster lines along the course. Again, unless you are out front on your own, do not use them all the time. Follow your rivals around the obvious but slower sections, and attack just before them, if possible getting a gap big enough so that when you do use the quicker route those following will not see you and follow.

Most cyclo-cross tactics presuppose that everybody is racing as an individual, but most people ride for a team, and if you have teammates in the race, tactics can be employed similar to those used on the road. If you find yourself with a teammate, attack and leave the rest to chase you with your teammate sitting in. If you are caught, he should attack immediately and leave you to police the chasers. Eventually, they will be unable to keep making the efforts required, and one of you will be able to stay clear.

When one of you manages to escape the clutches of the group, the other rider can still help by leading the group through any narrow sections ... but not at full speed. This will effectively break up the chase and slow the group, allowing the gap to widen.

So what happens if you are the one being attacked? How can you stop what has been described above from happening to you?

First, know your opponent. If you know someone is a good runner, make sure you are first off your bike at the beginning of the run, so that you can lead at your own pace. With a bike on your shoulder it is not too hard to keep somebody behind you, but watch out for the moment you remount, as this is an excellent time for him to try to get clear. If he gets his feet in quickly and accelerates away while the efforts of the run are still hampering you, a gap will appear, so stay alert.

If someone is riding a log you have to run, approach the obstacle in the lead and take it at your own pace. He will need a clear run to bunny-hop it, so take the opportunity to break up his rhythm.

Watch your opponents as they go through the pits. Are they taking a clean bike every lap? Are their bike changes good ones? Is it worth skipping a bike change to attack through the pit? This will depend on the state of the course and your bike, but bear it in mind — it might be just what they were not expecting you to do!

If you still find yourself in company at the end of the race and are resigned to a sprint finish, then make sure you are leading into the final obstacle, whether it is the last bend or a dismount, and lead out. It is rare for a cyclo-cross race to have a long finishing straight where you could employ road-sprint tactics. In the unlikely event of a sprint, it is usually the rider on the front approaching the finish who wins; ask the Italians beaten by Adri! ■

CHAPTER 7

TRAINING

Juvenile training

uvenile cycle racing is the place where most of the stars of today made their first appearances, whether in a circuit race on the road, a 'cross, a 10-mile evening time trial, or a local mountain bike race.

Juvenile and junior racing are the ideal places to learn cycle racing. But it is important not to specialize at an early age in one branch of the sport; you should try everything going. Even if as a senior rider you decide 'cross is for you, to compete at a high level you must be proficient on the road or mountain bike during the summer months. No longer can success be gained on a six-month season — ride as many juvenile races on the road, track, and mountain bike as you can. The experience will pay off later.

Most important of all, enjoy riding your bike. Training seriously, and the complicated business of training schedules, interval training, weights, and so on, should be left until you are a junior at least, or preferably a senior. By then you will have finished growing, gotten the business of study and exams out of the way, and can decide what sort of effort and commitment you want to put into your racing.

At the same time, do not limit your sporting involvement to cycling. Involve yourself in as many sports as you can while the facilities are available to you at school. All of them will help you with your cycling. A cyclo-cross rider needs to be able to do more than just ride a bike fast. He must be able to run, jump and carry a bike, and this requires more than just pure cycling can offer. All sports can be used to improve your athleticism.

If you are keen on 'cross and looking for success even at an early age, you should plan your program with great care; if possible, under the guidance of a coach.

Do not be quick to compare yourself with other riders of your age, or the training they do. Some people mature faster than others, and their success can be simply a result of their increased strength, while others who grow more slowly might find themselves slipping back in performance in relation to their friends or teammates. So results will be hard to compare.

It is probably easier for a late developer to continue with a cycling career than for someone who matured early and found success easily with little effort. By between the ages of 18 and 20, most people have grown to their full extent, and the people who have had early success have to increase their efforts significantly to stay ahead — or, as usually happens, training becomes too much effort, and they are lost to the sport.

The record books are full of juvenile and junior medal-winners who have faded away because the going got tough. But if you look further down the same result tables, you will find a lot of names who are now top riders, and who have found their success by hard work.

To come through the teenage years and continue as a cyclist is an achievement in itself. Cycling does not have the glamorous image of many other sports, and very few people can make a good living from it, compared to, say, football. It is also too easy to fall in with what the majority do. During school years, there is great pressure to be one of the crowd, not to follow an unusual individual sport. If you can make it through these years enjoying your cycling and learning what it is all about, and continue with a dedicated outlook, then the future for you will be bright.

Training for juvenile races should include a full range of sports. Within the context of cycling, the summers should be spent on "steady state" riding on the road or mountain bike, having fun and getting some miles in. Rides with a cycling club, weekends away on the bike and rides to local evening time trials or weekend mountain bike races are great ways to do this without thinking of it as training.

Ride time trials if they are available during the evenings in the week. Twenty-kilometer time trials are perfect; do a few 40km events, but nothing any longer; and don't be tempted into the search for fast courses to improve your times. These races teach you how to ride alone at speed — something you will have to do a lot of during a cyclo-cross — and how to concentrate.

On weekends, try to ride a mix of races: some criteriums or circuit races as a juvenile, and road races once you turn junior. These will teach you how to ride in a pack, and how to brake and corner. Also ride mountain bike races, as these will improve your bike-handling skills off-road, and are great fun!

In the winter, race as many weekends as you can. Most areas have local cyclo-cross races, many on Saturdays. By riding these, you can leave Sunday free for longer rides with your friends or cycling club, or maybe even another race if there is one close by.

During the week, do not train hard until you have recovered from your weekend's activities. As you will be at school, any training you do will be in the evenings, so make sure your bike has a good lighting system and that you can be seen. Many cycling clubs have some kind of midweek training ride, usually attended by road racers keeping an edge on their winter fitness with a brisk ride.

These are ideal for you, much better (and safer) than training alone. If you have difficulty keeping up for the full distance, go as far as you can with them until you get dropped, then ride home steadily. This way you will be able to gauge whether you are improving by seeing how far you get each week.

On other evenings find some well-lighted grassland — either a flood-lit sports field or some grass by a road — and practice your technique on your 'cross bike. Try to do this with a friend if possible, working on your basic skills — mounting and dismounting, getting your feet into the pedals quickly, and short stretches of running with your bike.

This training, combined with your school sports, will be adequate. Remember that all your training must be progressive, and you will not get results overnight.

You also should try to get into the habit of stretching daily to keep your muscles flexible. You are still growing, and this will reduce the likelihood of any growing pains due to contracted muscles.

Weight training should be avoided until you are fully mature, and even then done only under the supervision of a coach. However, circuit training is advisable if you can fit it in, either at home or in the school gym.

Pay attention to your diet, and follow the guidelines in the section on nutrition. Try to avoid too much candy, and do not ignore meals to fit in more training. If you are still growing, it is important to eat regularly and sensibly.

Training principles

If you have recently been introduced to cycling, you may be confused by what you have read concerning training routines, "levels" of training, heart-rate monitors ... the list goes on and on, and most of it takes a sports-science degree to comprehend.

In the good old days, people simply went out for rides, then raced on weekends. Well, welcome to the '90s! People still go out for rides, but the majority of people competing now want to know what it is exactly they are doing while training, and what effect it will have on their body and their racing results. Hey ... why train for 25 hours a week if you can achieve the same results in only 15 hours? Just think — 10 spare hours to spend in bed, watching TV or even doing some work!

The first thing you must realize about training is that every single one of us is different. And although principles of training apply in a broad physiological sense to everybody, the circumstances under which you carry out your training and your lifestyle will dictate to what extent certain principles work. You are not a lab rat.

For this reason, if you read in a magazine interview that the Swiss guy who won the big race last month trains behind a motorcycle for four hours each Wednesday morning, do not be tempted to rush out and try to do the same. In the first place, you would probably crawl home, absolutely shattered, after an hour or so. And in the second place, you would have doubts about how you are ever going to make the grade if you can't even cope with just one day of a top pro's schedule!

So rule No. 1 is: Never copy anybody else's training routine, especially the good guys. They have evolved their training routines over the years and gradually accustomed their bodies to the stresses involved. To jump in at the deep end as a novice will simply be too much, physically and mentally, and you will not be able to continue for very long.

The four levels of training

In the following sections, I will refer to "levels" of training to simplify training routines. These four basic levels have been established from the results of laboratory exercise tests, covering every level of intensity and duration. By using these levels, structuring your training becomes very simple.

You can base this training on heart rate (HR) to give you a clearer picture of how hard you are really working. If you don't have a heart-rate monitor and cannot afford to buy one, don't worry. See if you can borrow one, or share the cost among a group of friends. You only need to use one for a short period to get a feel for certain heart rates and how you feel at those heart rates. After a while, you will be able to gauge the rate you are training at even when you don't have the monitor.

First, you need to determine your threshold HR, as it is from this rate that the training levels are based. The threshold HR is the rate that your heart beats during efficient aerobic effort, when the production of lactic acid (the waste product produced in your muscles) is equal to the speed that it is removed by the body. In simple terms, this is the rate your heart beats at when you are going flat out over a 20-30 minute ride; say, during a 20km time trial.

Use the HR monitor for a time trial, either in competition or training, and make a mental note of your heart rate during the middle section of the ride — from 10 to 20 minutes is best. This will give you a very accurate measure of your threshold HR, and from this you will see how to train at the four main levels.

Levels

- Level 1: Rides of three to four hours in duration; long, steady distance (LSD).
- Level 2: Rides of one hour to 90 minutes in duration.
- Level 3: Intense training sessions of 20-30 minutes.
- Level 4: Interval training. Repeated efforts of up to three minutes in duration.
- Recovery: Easy riding, not a training session.

Level 1

- Intensity: Best described as a brisk pace, with breathing just at the point of becoming noticeable (deep and regular).
- Heart rate: Approximately threshold minus 25 beats per minute.
- Duration: Three to four hours (full); one to two hours (short).
- Frequency: One session per week (occasionally two if time allows).
- Effects: Improves fuel supply, as it trains most of the fibers in a muscle to use a fatty fuel mixture. Also provides some training of the oxygen-transport system.
- Hints: Best performed in small groups. Attempt to maintain a constant pace. Correct carbohydrate feeding is important both during and immediately after the session (see "Carbohydrate supplements," Page 138).

Level 2

- Intensity: Best described as "comfortably hard." Breathing rate and depth are noticeably higher than at Level 1. Conversation is possible, but frequent pauses to regain breathing pattern are necessary.
- Heart rate: Approximately threshold minus 15 beats per minute.
- Duration: One hour to 90 minutes.
- Frequency: Two sessions per week.
- Effects: Trains a fair proportion of the muscle fibers to use a mixture of carbohydrate and fat, and provides moderate training of the oxygen-transport system.
- Hints: Best performed as controlled "two-up" training, with two riders taking turns pulling. Use varied terrain where possible. For any

rides over one hour, adequate fluid and carbohydrate intake during and after training is essential.

Level 3

- Intensity: Very high. Virtually the same as riding a 20km time trial. Breathing rapid and deep. Requires intense concentration.
- Heart rate: Approximately threshold minus five beats per minute.
- Duration: No longer than 30 minutes.
- Frequency: One session per week.
- Effects: Trains most muscle fibers, and uses mainly carbohydrate as a fuel. This is a high level of training for the oxygen-transport system. It accustoms the body to the physical load that will be encountered during a race.
- Hints: Vary the terrain. Begin the session with a 30-minute warm-up, and get into the right frame of mind. Possible to ride as a "two-up" effort. A good session on a turbo-trainer.

Level 4

- Intensity: Near maximal. Breathing very rapid and uncomfortable. Physically and psychologically very demanding.
- Heart rate: Heart rates are not a good guide for this type of training, as it is non-steady state.
- Duration: Short intervals, 10-30 seconds; medium intervals, 45-60 seconds; long intervals, 90 seconds to three minutes. Rest interval should be long enough to recover from the effort (about three to five minutes).
- Frequency: One session per week.
- Effects: Trains virtually all fibers in a muscle, and uses solely carbohydrate as a fuel. Best possible training of the oxygen-transport system.
- Hints: Best performed alone, either on a turbo-trainer or on varied terrain. Warm up thoroughly.

Since each level indicates how many times a week you should perform a particular session, drawing up a training plan is very simple. However, you must decide yourself, or preferably with the aid of a coach, how much time you are prepared to devote to training before sitting down and working out your plan.

As most people can't train full time, and must fit in training and racing around work and family commitments, we shall take a look at how that can be done.

Training around a working day

Every racer would love to be able to train and rest full time, but unless you are prepared to sacrifice everything in pursuit of your sport, the chances are that you will be working. Unless you are in a position to work shifts or "flex-time," you will also have to contend with doing most of your training in the dark. But if you are keen to improve and dedicated in your approach, this and the discomforts of training in winter weather must be overcome.

The first thing you must do is sit down and work out the time you have available to train, and any other commitments you have apart from work. A single person may be able to devote more time to training than someone with a a family, for instance.

The time you have available in an evening will probably not amount to much more than an hour to 90 minutes, but this is as much as is required for one session. Take a look at the rest of your day. Is it possible to fit in a 20-minute run before work, or a turbo-trainer session in your lunch hour? If the answer is "yes," then suddenly you have the ability to fit in a three-session day every now and again — total time, two to two and a half hours — which is just fine.

If you are limited to the hour at the end of the day, it is not the end of the world — you will simply have to go for quality instead of quantity. Provided you can build up a reasonable base of longer rides during the longer evenings in the summer, and over the weekends, you will have the basis of a good regime for cyclo-cross racing.

If time is tight or the weather is so bad that you cannot face going out on the bike, then you have two alternatives: hop on the turbo-trainer for

a session; or go for a run. Running is easier to fit in than riding, and is
not such a chore in very bad weather ... although you should never
venture out when it is icy or foggy as it becomes too much of a health
risk. On such days, stick to the turbo, or create a circuit of stretching and
indoor exercises.

As with all training, it should be progressive, with gradual increases in quality as the season progresses and the bigger races approach. It
is important to have periods of rest to recover mentally from the pressures of training hard, and to keep a careful check on your health; be
alert for any hints your body may provide that you may be doing too
much too soon.

Your training should work in cycles of three or four weeks followed
by an easier week. The next cycle should be progressively harder, and
so on. If you start in September, following the gradual build-up over the
summer, you will go through four or five "cycles" before the end of
the season in February.

If we presume you can fit in two sessions a day totaling 90 minutes, here are examples of the five cycles or phases you could base
your training on around a working day.

Phase 1 — September

Three weeks' training followed by one week's rest.

Daily stretching exercises; record your waking heart rate each morning and your weight each week.

Monday-Thursday

a.m.: 20-minute run, steady, on grass.

p.m.: One-hour road ride (Level 2).

Replace one evening session with circuit training if available.

Friday

Rest, or 1-hour recovery ride.

Saturday

90 minutes, cyclo-cross on a circuit if available, with 30 minutes practicing techniques, and 45-60 minutes on the circuit (upper Level 2).

Sunday

Two- to three-hour road ride (Level 1). Hilly if possible.

Rest week

The purpose of the rest week is to recover from the previous three weeks and to prepare mentally for the increased efforts of the next phase. Do not force yourself to train during this week. If the weather is bad, or you do not feel like going out, take a break.

Try to train on three of the weekdays as described below, to ensure you don't lose any fitness. Stretch daily; record your waking HR each morning, and your weight at the end of the week.

Monday-Friday

At least two 20-minute runs and three one-hour Level 1 road rides during the week.

Saturday-Sunday

90-minute Level 2 road rides both days.

Phase 2 — October

Three weeks' training followed by one rest week as in Phase 1.

Monday

One-hour road ride (L1).

Tuesday

a.m.: 20-minute run, grass.

p.m.: One-hour road ride (L2).

Wednesday

a.m.: 20-minute run, grass.

p.m.: 30-minute road or turbo workout (L3). (Don't forget 30 mins. warm-up).

Thursday

Repeat Tuesday's workouts.

Friday

Rest, or 45-60 minute recovery ride.

Saturday

Two-hour road ride (L1).

Sunday

Race.

Phase 3 — November

Three week's training followed by one rest week, as in Phases 1-2. Stretch daily; record waking HR each morning and weight each week.

Monday

One-hour road ride (L1).

Tuesday

a.m.: 25-minute run, grass (hard L3).

p.m.: One-hour road ride (upper L2).

Wednesday

a.m.: Intervals session on turbo-trainer. Five-minute warm-up followed by five 30-second intervals at maximum, with two minutes' recovery between each.

p.m.: One-hour road ride (L1).

Thursday

a.m.: 20-minute run, grass (L2).

p.m.: 30-minute road or turbo workout (L3).

Friday

Rest or 45-60 minutes recovery ride.

Saturday

Race.

Sunday

Race.

Phase 4 — December

Three weeks' training followed by one rest week. Also race as much as possible over the Christmas and New Year period, but modify training around this time to suit. Stretch daily; record waking HR each morning and weight each week.

Monday

60- to 90-minute road ride (L1).

Tuesday

a.m.: 30 minutes running — 10-min. warm-up; 10-min. intervals (100m uphill, with jog down to recover); and 10-min. jog to warm down.

p.m.: One-hour road ride (L2).

Wednesday

a.m.: Turbo-trainer session — 10-minute warm-up, then 20 minutes. (L3)

p.m.: 'Cross skills session, one hour.

Thursday

a.m. 25-minute run (steady L1), including 5 x 1 min. intervals (hard L3).

p.m.: One-hour road ride (L1), including 10 x 100m sprints (L4) out of corners, uphills, etc.

Friday

Rest or 45-60 minutes recovery ride.

Saturday

Race.

Sunday

Race.

Phase 5 — January

Four weeks' training followed by one rest week. Stretch daily; record waking pulse each morning and weight each week.

Monday

60- to 90-minute road ride (L1).

Tuesday

a.m.: 30-minute run — 10 mins. warm-up; 10-mins. intervals (100m uphill [L4] with jog down to recover) and 10 mins. jogging to warm down.

p.m.: One-hour road ride (upper L2), including 10 x 150m sprints (L4), out of corners, uphills, etc.

Wednesday

a.m.: Turbo session — 10 mins. warm-up, then 20 mins. (L3).

p.m.: One hour on 'cross circuit (L2).

Thursday

a.m.: 25-minute run (L1), including 3 x 3 min. intervals (L3).

p.m.: One-hour road ride (L2).

Friday

Rest or 45-60 minutes recovery ride.

Saturday

Race.

Sunday

Race.

Notes

Saturday races should be small, local races. But if Sunday's race is an important one, then Saturday's race should be replaced by a one-hour road ride at Level 1.

Interval training is very hard, both mentally and physically. If at any time you have not recovered from a previous session (the best way to tell this is a waking HR more than five beats higher or lower than normal), you should replace the interval session with a recovery ride.

If you cannot discipline yourself to set intervals, replace them with fartlek training. Fartlek, meaning "speed play," is used by runners to give variety to their training. Sprint for signs, trees, lampposts, to the top of a hill or down the other side. Without setting times or distances, fartlek still incorporates all the benefits of an interval session. Always allow time for a warm-up and warm-down. Never start an interval session unless you have warmed up for at least 15 minutes (10 minutes if running).

Start each day with a full routine of stretching, and also stretch gently before each training session or race.

If you are forced to miss a day's training due to bad weather, illness or weariness, do not be tempted into doing more the next day. Stick to your schedule. Complete your training diary, and note how you feel. You can refer back to this to explain any changes in your form.

Do not be tied down to these or any other schedules. If you feel you are not ready to move on to the next stage, carry on with the one you are on. Also, do not be afraid to taper your training prior to an important race.

Around Christmas and the New Year, depending how the days fall, it is usually possible to race a number of times — and you should take advantage of this, as it is an excellent way to bring your form to a peak for the big races in January and February.

Do not train hard between these races; just keep to steady rides. Keep an eye on what your body is telling you, and if you have not recovered fully, give the next day's race a miss.

On Fridays, you will notice that these schedules give you a choice between total rest and a steady ride. I favor total rest, but many people prefer a steady ride. If you cannot face the bike come Friday, keep off it; if you fancy a ride, go for it ... but keep it steady.

Rest

The most important part of a good training regime is ... resting!

The purpose of training is to place your body under physical stress over time, so it will adapt to the stresses imposed upon it and increase its ability to cope with greater stresses in the future. But your body needs time to adapt itself to the stress of training if it is to be of any benefit, and this comes in the form of rest.

Pros always take enough rest. When was the last time you saw a pro rushing around, or riding around the car park at a race, popping wheelies? They don't do these sorts of things — mostly, they sit down a lot!

The need for rest is even greater if you work full time, so you need to make sure it is a major part of your schedule. If you haven't been training long, taking two days a week off is a good idea; Monday and Friday are the best, both physically and mentally. Physically, it is good to have consecutive days of hard work. And mentally, taking Friday off helps you prepare for a good weekend of training or racing after a hard week, while resting again on Monday ensures you are recovered before you resume training on Tuesday.

Overtraining

Doing too much is just as bad for you as not doing enough training — especially too much high-intensity stuff without enough recovery. If you get to the stage where you are training hard but your performances are going downhill, it's time to look for signs of overtraining.

The best indicator is your resting heart rate. As you have already seen, if you note a variation of five beats above or below the normal rate, you know something is wrong, so take it easy. Other signs are a disturbed sleep pattern, a depressed appetite and a general feeling of irritability or depression. Also, if you train with a HR monitor and cannot reach a high HR during intervals or Level 3 training, then you are overtired.

If you catch it early, a couple of days taking things easy will set everything right. If you continue battering yourself and get chronic overtraining symptoms, it will take more than a couple of days to go away. You need a good break to recover (a week or perhaps longer), and then you can start building back up ... very slowly.

With time, athletes become very highly tuned to their bodies and what their bodies are telling them. It is important to realize how you are feeling all the time, and what conditions make you feel differently. In this way, you can forestall overuse injuries, illnesses and overtraining — all of which can become major problems if not caught early enough, resulting in lost time and training while you recover.

Using a turbo-trainer

The turbo-trainer has become an almost essential piece of equipment for the racing cyclist, especially those who want to train or compete during the winter.

Although there is an ever-increasing number of makes and designs on the market, the basic principle is the same; that is, to create a resistance on the rear wheel while pedaling. The choice of trainer, while suiting the budget of the buyer, can also depend on the space available, or just personal preference. There are a number of portable and fold-up designs on the market, and these can be especially useful to take to races to warm up on before a race.

Turbo-trainers that incorporate a fan and flywheel are recommended as they provide a smooth ride and the resistance increases as the effective rear wheel speed increases. One disadvantage is that these can sometimes be a little noisy to use, so it helps if you have understanding neighbors!

Trainers that incorporate a magnetic resistance unit are a lot quieter and have fixed increments of resistance, but this is reflected in the price. As a general guide, if you are going to use the trainer regularly in one place and the space is available, then a rigid system with a fan and flywheel is best. If space is limited and you wish to take the trainer to events, then the foldaway, A-frame-design units are best. And, with a magnetic resistance unit, it can be used for warming up in the hotel lobby or even training in the room, keeping noise to a minimum.

Advantages of a turbo-trainer

Possibly the greatest advantage is that it is 100-percent safe for any interval training, as you need not look where you are going, or watch for traffic. You can also control your heart-rate zone more efficiently for longer periods of work, as there are no breaks in your momentum, such as you would experience on the open road with hills, head winds, stop lights, traffic, and so on. As such, you have complete control over your training, with no influence from external factors such as darkness or bad weather.

Disadvantages of a turbo-trainer

Compared to the advantages, they are few. But long sessions can be mind-numbingly dull without something to watch or listen to. A video of your favorite race can be inspiring; a favorite CD in the portable stereo can help pass the time. The better models of trainer are programmable with race courses and display a full range of information, such as power output, HR, RPM and speed, to keep your interest up.

If you do not have a fan or are in a badly ventilated area, then training can become very uncomfortable. So make sure you invest in a fan, and have a water spray bottle on hand to wet your face — scientific evidence has suggested increased efficiency and tolerance to warm climates from facial wetting.

The only other potential, if unlikely, disadvantage is that you may become reliant on the trainer for training, and not want to go outside in the cold to ride. While turbo-training has its place for controlling safe, high-intensity workouts, it is only a substitute — training must also be performed in an environment that approximates racing conditions.

Turbo-training hints

Before we talk about training, here are a few tips to keep in mind. Don't overdress for a training session; shorts and an under-vest will be enough, with possibly an extra jersey to start with if you are in an unheated garage.

The area where you train should be well-ventilated and not too warm; open a door or window to get a draft. A temperature above 68 degrees Fahrenheit (20°C) is too hot, so keep away from any sources of heat, such as radiators.

You will need a large cooling fan if you are going to train indoors, as overheating can have serious consequences, affecting training levels and target heart rates.

You should also have a drinking bottle handy while training, and always make sure you are well-hydrated before you start a session.

If you train in a garage or outbuilding, make sure the floor is free of dust — the trainer's fan will blow it all around, and you'll end up inhaling it; not a good idea.

Turbo-training workouts

Although the cyclo-cross rider will use the turbo mainly for high-intensity workouts, it also can be employed for endurance or long, steady distance work. Don't forget, you need this LSD before you can embark on any shorter, faster sessions.

- Endurance work: If the weather forces you to stay indoors for your endurance session, then typically you would expect to warm up for five minutes, followed by an hour at Level 2, followed by a five-minute warm-down.
- Strength and power sessions: These workouts are of a higher training intensity and shorter duration, and are aimed at improving your ability to maintain a speed just above race pace for short periods. This typically occurs in a cyclo-cross race when you make your starting effort, or are attacking other riders.

Once again, warm-up for five minutes, then do 25 to 30 minutes of intervals at a HR just above Level 3. Start with three minutes at high L3, followed by one minute of recovery, and repeat five times. If this becomes too easy after a while, increase the work interval's duration to four minutes, or increase the number of intervals to six.

An alternative to this is a "pyramid" session, in which you increase the duration of the work interval up to a point, then decrease it toward the end of the session. It is particularly good for developing your strength, and mimics the effort common to the middle of a race, when attacks and counters are at their thickest.

Start with a one-minute work interval at L3 with one minute of recovery. Then increase each subsequent work interval by 30 seconds until you reach a three-minute work interval. At that point, reduce each successive interval by 30 seconds until you are back at one minute, and the session is completed. You will have completed 17 minutes of intervals, plus eight minutes of recoveries; total time, 25 minutes. When this becomes easy, add another interval at the top.

- Speed endurance: As the season gets serious, you will be looking to improve your speed endurance — that is, your ability to make repeated fast efforts over short distances of around 400 meters.

This training typically involves making repeated efforts with short recovery times in between. As you adapt to these sessions, you should aim to reduce the recovery time and increase the number of work intervals. These sessions should last only about 20 minutes, but are performed at the top end of your Level 3 training zone.

After the normal warm-up, do one-minute intervals with one minute of recovery, repeated 10 times. As you adapt to the stress, add an interval and reduce the recovery periods by five seconds so that you have 11 x 1 minute intervals with 10 recoveries of 55 seconds.

- Tapering before championships: When your training comes to a peak before the season-ending championship races, you need to taper. This means very short intervals at maximum intensity, with relatively little recovery.

A session like this will typically consist of six to 10 repetitions of around one minute, maximum, with one minute of recovery. When you can complete 10 intervals, reduce the recovery time by 10 seconds, then start at six intervals, or more if you can do it. When you can manage 10 again, reduce the recovery by 10 seconds and the number of intervals to six, and so on.

As you approach the tapering-down period in the couple of weeks before the big race, try reducing the interval time to 30 seconds with a 30-second recovery. Again, when you can manage 10 intervals, reduce the recovery to 20 seconds and start at six intervals, repeating the procedure as above.

Stretching

As we have emphasized, one aspect of your training routine that should never be missed is your daily dose of stretching. You can recognize the cyclists who don't stretch; they hobble around as if they have just got off their bikes after a hard, 100-mile ride, or have just aged prematurely.

Cycling keeps your muscles in a contracted state, meaning that your arms, legs and back do not operate through their full range of movements. It is important that this is remedied off the bike through a comprehensive routine of stretches to avoid injury, and to lessen the risk of muscular strains and soreness. A good stretch can also have the same effect as a massage, removing waste from the muscles and helping recovery.

You should stretch before and after a training session; first thing in the morning (especially if you run then); and before bed if you feel stiff after a hard day's training. It doesn't take long — only a matter of minutes per session — and should become a routine.

Those riders we mentioned earlier, hobbling around — take a look at them on their bike, and I'll bet they don't look quite right. They usually appear to be sitting too low and too far forward, riding on the front of the saddle. A lack of mobility means that they cannot pedal in the most efficient position on the bike, so they set the bike up in a fashion that feels comfortable, but actually adds to their problems. Still, you stretch, your position is right, and you beat them anyway, so what do you care?

Hints for effective stretching

- Do not stretch too far. Produce a slight stretch, and hold it at that point for around 30 seconds. The point of stretch should never be painful.
- Never bounce. Bouncing tightens the very muscles you are trying to stretch, so stretch gently and hold it.
- Breathe slowly and deeply. Concentrate on the muscle you are stretching, and relax.
- Never rush a set of stretches.
- Do not try to match yesterday's efforts. You will be naturally stiffer or looser on some days than on others.
- Do not compare yourself with others — everybody is different

and has different levels of flexibility.

• Regular stretching is the key. Little and often is better than a lot every now and then.

Stretching routine

This should be carried out as regularly as possible, but always before and after training, and any time you have a spare moment.

Use the following as a guide, and add your own stretches as you go on. Initially, as you develop the routine, start at your head and work down. This will help you not to forget any body part.

People tend to spend more time on the first leg, arm or area they stretch, and they usually stretch their "easy" or more flexible side first. To even out the differences in flexibility in your body, stretch your tight side first.

Weight training

Weight training for the cyclo-cross rider can become a useful and enjoyable part of the workout schedule, as it is the best way to isolate and strengthen certain muscles that fatigue quickly. These muscles are not worked in isolation when cycling, but as a group, and will not strengthen significantly as a result of cycling alone. The best examples are your forearms, upper arms, shoulders and back, all of which at times can ache as much as your legs during and after a hard race!

Decide for yourself how much weight training you need. For instance, if you have a manual-labor job, you will probably not need to strengthen your arms and shoulders. But if you sit at a desk all day, then you probably could do with some extra work.

Nowadays, it is not necessary to use free weights, which in the hands of a beginner can be awkward and even unsafe. The technology of multi-gyms means that any muscle can be worked on a machine without the risk of injury from the inexperienced use of free weights.

Work out a weight-training program with the aid of an experienced person, such as an instructor in a gym. Explain what it is you are trying to achieve, and the instructor will plan a program to include all the appropriate body parts. All the exercises will be performed to increase the muscular endurance of each body part, so you will perform a high number of repetitions at a relatively low weight. Muscular power, developed by using heavy weights with few repetitions, is not for you. You are not looking to become a body builder on a bike!

You should try to fit in a session of weights at least twice a week — three times, if possible, for the best effect — and continue throughout the season. If after a race you notice that one body part is more tired or aching more than any other, then concentrate on building up the strength of that part.

Weight training has to be progressive to work. Don't perform the same exercises week in, week out, at the same weight and same number of repetitions. Start at a comfortable weight, at which you can perform three sets of 15 repetitions. Then do two sets of 15 reps and one of 20; then one of 15 and two of 20; then three of 20. When you can do that, increase the weight and drop back to three sets of 15 reps.

If you cannot manage 15 reps of an exercise, the weight is too heavy, so reduce it. Don't worry; your strength will increase quite quickly in the early stages ... and you won't be using the bar with no weights on it for long!

Weight-training exercises

Use the following exercises as the basis for your program, and add your own, depending on what machines are available in the gym and what your instructor advises.

Always start with a thorough warm-up, consisting of your stretching routine, followed by five minutes on an exercise bike or running machine. Afterward, have a gentle pedal on the stationary bike to warm down, and gently stretch any muscles that feel tight.

1. Inner thigh
2. Outer thigh
3. Leg extensions, single
4. Leg curls, single or double
5. Calf raises
6. Bench press, lying or seated
7. Pulldowns, standing or sitting

8. Lateral raises

9. Triceps pushdown

10. Upright rowing

In addition to the above, you can supplement your program with the following;

11. Sit-ups

12. Back hyperextensions

13. Chin-ups

14. Hanging leg raises, which don't require the use of weights

Circuit training

As an all-round fitness training regime, circuit training is highly recommended. If time allows, it can be carried out both pre-season and in-season.

Circuit training comprises a number of exercises in a gym — some using apparatus, others not — that exercise different groups of muscles and the cardiovascular system. Each exercise is performed in turn, usually for one minute, during which time you attempt to do as many repetitions of the exercise as possible. After a brief, timed rest (usually the same as your effort time while a partner performs the exercises), you move on to the next one, and so on, usually for 10 to 12 exercises. The complete circuit is then repeated a second or third time ... depending on the fitness of the participants!

Make no mistake: Circuit training done properly is exhausting. If it isn't, either you are not trying hard enough or the recovery time is too long. After an initial session of stretching and jogging to warm up, followed by the circuits and a warm-down, you will have probably spent an hour working — but the effects will feel like much more!

Circuits are best done in pairs, one resting while the other works. This also introduces a competitive element into the training, as scores can be compared.

A number of cycling clubs introduce circuit training classes during the winter, but if no clubs in your area have a class, try a local sports center. If you still draw a blank, it is possible to make a home circuit using the exercises that do not require apparatus. But you must be strict with the timing of the effort and recovery periods, as it is too easy to cheat when unsupervised!

So you want to be world champion ...

Every cyclist has ambition. That ambition may be to improve on a previous best time in a club time trial, to become the area road-race champion, or to win the local cyclo-cross series. When this step has been achieved, it is natural to want to move up a step, to set goals that you feel you can achieve within the circumstances in which you find yourself.

If you have a family and work, the consequent restrictions on your time may mean that your ambition cannot be fulfilled. You may have to accept that you can reach a certain level and go no further, being happy to compete at that level.

Success may come easily; you may be a particularly gifted rider who, without too much effort, has made his way through the rankings to become a member of the national team. Some riders reach this level and consider they have made it. Year in, year out, they are happy to put in enough work to justify their position, to perform well in their own country and be the big fish in the little pond.

Occasional trips to compete abroad against a better class of rider at, say, the world championships, usually yield disappointing results. But as they are "foreign," and it's a big sport in their country, you expect them to be good and make no further effort to bridge the gap.

If that is where your ambitions lie, then fine. You will be successful, gain respect as a rider and enjoy your racing and trips. But every now and then, especially toward the end of your racing career, you will start to wonder what might have been "if only...." If only you had moved to Belgium for a winter before you settled down and got married; if only you had taken notice of the national coach when he told you that a talent like yours shouldn't be wasted; if only you had made a bit more effort for world's selection that year you were going well; yeah, yeah, yeah.

Every so often a rider comes along who, after reaching this level, sits down and thinks, "Right ... where do I go from here?" Ambition does not stop with a national title, because he or she wants more. Perhaps a ride in a world championship sparks a desire to be world champion, and it is then that the even harder work starts.

In countries such as the United States and Britain, very few people have made that decision, and despite recent signs of improvement, they have not been a force to be reckoned with in international cyclo-cross. Still, it only takes a couple of people to start making the grade on the world scene for a whole country's racing to improve — the rest of the domestic riders must improve to keep up. Success breeds success.

But what makes a champion? All cyclists can develop the four attributes required to be a good cyclist: skill, stamina, strength and speed. But champions have something extra that puts them above mere mortals — something that cannot be defined, a certain "class," a certain determination that makes them something special.

The physical attributes can be developed by hard, systematic training, and anyone with the motivation can fulfill their potential. But it is that certain something that makes the super-champion, and if you have got it, you owe it to yourself to go for it and see how far up the ladder you can get.

If you want to become a top cyclo-cross rider, you must be prepared to work hard and make sacrifices. Instead of fitting your training around your circumstances, you must change your circumstances to fit your training and racing.

At the top level, 'cross, like every other sport, is a full-time occupation. Your world revolves around training, eating, sleeping and racing. Your time for a social life is limited, and when it is available, you are usually too tired to take advantage of it. It is no longer a six-month-a-year sport. All the top 'cross stars are inevitably top mountain-bike or road riders in their own right, and compete on the world stage for 10 months a year.

Riders like Frischknecht, Djernis, Pontoni, Luca Bramati and Mike Kluge are capable of winning at any discipline at any time of the year ... but remember, they all began their winning ways as 'cross riders. Even the so-called 'cross specialists, who number fewer and fewer each year as mountain bike racing takes up so much time during the summer, are still preparing for their winter season on the roads or on fat tires. The fact that they concentrate their efforts on 'cross is usually due to some lucrative sponsorship or salary-boosting prize money being available.

So if it is going to be so hard, why bother? At all levels of competition, 'cross can be psychologically rewarding, but at the top it can be financially rewarding and provide international acclaim. However, in the end, it could just come down to you not wanting to bore your partner in your old age with constant reminiscing about how "if only..."!

High-level training

The sections that follow deal with training at a high level. You will see that they don't leave much time for work! If your situation means that all this training is not possible for you, you should seek your coach's advice in order to decide what is best, and then work out a schedule. Use the suggestions below as an outline in order to cover every aspect of training, and work out what is best for you.

Remember that training must be progressive. If you are presently only training for 10 hours a week, do not try to double it to 20 hours straight away. Your body will not be able to cope with it, and you will wear yourself out quickly. Gradually build up the hours, and when you can cope with the time involved, then — and only then — start to increase the intensity of the efforts. No intense or interval training should be attempted until a solid background of LSD work has been achieved.

Running

Running plays a part in 'cross races, and every rider has to run at some point in races, so it makes sense to run during training. But with the recent trend in race circuits, toward faster races with fewer long runs, the importance of heavy running sessions has dropped a little.

However, some riders feel the benefits of regular running even on the bike, and as a high-quality Level 3 or 4 session, it cannot be faulted. Even if your running only takes place in the pre-season build-up, then fades away as more on-the-bike training takes over, it will still have been worth it.

Just in case you decide you don't need to run in training, remember that large crowds congregate on the big run-ups, and you can look really cool if you make it up at the front!

Running is a superb way in itself to improve the cardiovascular system. But the most important goal of your running program should be the ability to run well during a race. The runs you need to be able to perform in a race are likely to be short and sharp — either up a hill or over a piece of ground that is too muddy to ride. Your running training needs to reflect this, and be based on short and sharp efforts. But, of course, this cannot be done unless you have that base of running miles. In this way, it is similar to cycling.

All your running should be on grass if possible, or at least on a smooth surface. The jarring effect of running on roads makes the supple muscles of a cyclist very sore, and injuries can develop easily. If you are running cross-country, make sure that your footwear is up to the conditions.

If bad weather during the winter keeps you off your bike, then substitute a session of running. In a half-hour run, you can do as much work as in a much longer bike ride. Bad weather is not such a problem with running, as you are generating a lot of heat, and are out for a relatively short time.

Running should not be attempted without a good warm-up, especially if done first thing in the morning, as a lot of training plans suggest.

Running training should start in August, with three sessions a week. Start with a leisurely 15 minutes, then build up to 45-60 minutes at a steady Level 1 pace by the end of September.

In October, you should start on a schedule that will take you through the season. You should try to run for 25 minutes on Tuesday, Wednesday, and Thursday mornings ... and, it is hoped, you will be covering considerably more distance than you were going in August! Otherwise, not much should change with this schedule as the season progresses; only the intensity will increase as you become faster.

Interval work during these runs is not really necessary, as you will be getting enough L4 training in your turbo-training and 'cross sessions to simulate the efforts of a race. Doing large amounts of L4 training is not a good idea; it is hard mentally, so keep your daily runs enjoyable, but still fairly fast.

If you are of the opinion that running training costs you speed on the bike then give it a miss after the beginning of October. Simply do the initial pre-season runs to help get you in shape, and the specific running with your bike during the 'cross sessions will be adequate. Just bear in mind — if you start losing races or get dropped on any running section, however short, then you should look seriously at making running a more permanent part of your schedule.

Cyclo-cross training

Actual on-the-rough cyclo-cross training should start as your summer race season starts to wind down. If you compete on the mountain bike circuit, then you have had a summer of riding off-road, so there is no real hurry. You'll need a gentle reminder of the things that you can do on a mountain bike that you cannot do on a 'cross bike, but a couple of falls will soon refresh your memory!

If you only ride on the road during the summer, you need to start a little earlier — say, in mid-September — to re-acquaint yourself with the techniques required and sharpen up the skills before you start any serious training on your 'cross bike.

If you live in an area where the terrain is available, three- to four-hour rides on 'cross bikes in a small group are a tremendous way of getting into shape while working on specific skills, and they are great fun. If you are stuck in an area where this is not possible, replace this training with long road rides, preferably as hilly as possible. You should try to fit these rides in twice a week during September.

Once into October, all your 'cross training should take place on a smaller circuit, but not so small that you get bored training on it for an hour. A circuit that takes six to 10 minutes to complete is ideal. Your 'cross sessions will incorporate quite an amount of L4 work, and if this is done on the same circuit, then you can gauge your progress during the season.

When the season begins, your 'cross training does not need to last for more than one hour. With 10-15 minutes each for warm-up and warm-down, this leaves 30-40 minutes for the hard efforts, which should be varied from day to day to avoid the risk of boredom creeping in. Vary the circuits on certain days, or reverse the direction of Tuesday's circuit for Thursday's workout, and stick to these circuits all season.

You should always try to time your intervals and recoveries. Unless your coach can do this, which is ideal, use a sports watch with a stop-watch mode, or the stopwatch on your HR monitor.

The lengths of interval/recovery should always be recorded in your training diary for future reference. By doing this, it is easier to work out when to reduce the times and intensify the efforts.

Road training

Road training is a year-round occupation and the mainstay of your training routine, whether you race 'cross, road, track or mountain bike. Even though it is a year-round regime, you should vary it according to the time of year, the races you are preparing for and the stage you are at in your training "cycle."

No two weeks will be exactly the same, unless you are spending some time building a base of long, steady distance miles. And even this should be built up steadily over a four- or five-week cycle followed by an easier "rest" week.

After a break from the summer season of road or mountain biking, you should resume building up the training, ideally by mid-September to mid-October. Rides at this time of year should be based around the two- to three-hour mark, but by the time you get into the swing of the season and start racing in mid-October, most of the sessions you do will be closer to two or two and a half hours.

As the season progresses, you will reduce the actual time you spend on the road, although many riders still have one long day per week, riding for around three hours.

Once you get into the New Year, avoid the temptation to train with the road racers who have just awakened from their winter slumbers and are beginning to get the miles in. It might be nice and sociable, but it will not do much for your end-of-season goals in January and February.

A very effective way to train, if it is accessible to you, is behind a small motorcycle. A large number of professional riders use "paced" training, and as an aid to increased speed and condition it is unbeatable. A motorcycle can be used in two main ways: steady-state riding at a very high intensity (say, a two-hour L3 ride); or as an interval session, where the motorcycle is used as a "rabbit" to chase. This is a great way to stay focused — you try to stay with the pacer as it gradually increases the speed on the flat, or keeps a steady pace up gradual climbs.

Rest revisited

We have already touched on the importance of rest in conjunction with training on a daily basis. However, it is important to incorporate rest as part of your plan for the entire year, too.

Training in "cycles" of a number of weeks followed by a "rest" period gives both a physical break and an equally important mental respite. Blocks of four to five weeks are ideal, followed by a relatively easy week. In this way, you can tell yourself, "Only one more hard week, and then it's time for a break...." It's a bit like counting down the last few intervals in a session!

To make efforts 52 weeks a year is not possible for even the most committed person. Sometimes you need to lock the bike away and go do something else to stop yourself from going stale. For most riders, the best time to have a prolonged break is straight after the end of the season in mid-February. This should give you a three- or four-week period of relative relaxation before pre-summer training camps start. Another break at summer's end is also advisable.

These longer breaks, with seven or eight easier weeks of training at regular intervals, should keep you fresh and motivated all year 'round. The easier weeks do not mean no bike riding; they simply mean no strictly regimented plan. If you don't feel like riding, don't go out. If the sun is shining and you feel like a three-hour ride, then do it. For a few days, the mental strain of watching the clock, waiting for the next session, wondering if the rain will stop, is lifted. Stay in bed a bit longer; go out a couple of nights; switch off for a while.

Physically, you won't lose too much, especially if you put in the occasional unstructured workout; you won't get fitter, though, so don't make it habit-forming! Mentally, the respites will do you a world of good, and you will enter the next phase of your training plan raring to go.

Road and mountain bike racing for the cyclo-cross international

Nowadays, a mix of road and mountain bike racing should figure in the program of every 'cross racer, to improve strength, speed and skill. The likelihood is that you came into 'cross via the road or mountain bike anyway, and it just happened that you ended up with 'cross as your major interest, so you will know what is involved and what it is all about.

If you haven't ridden the road in a past life, then you will probably be a Cat. 4 or 5 racer. The majority of road races for this class will be 40-60 miles, and you should try to race these whenever possible. Also do as many criteriums as you can, as they require a very similar kind of effort to a cyclo-cross, with constant changes of pace into and out of corners.

If you are an experienced Cat. 2 or 3 road rider, then you will know the score and be in a better position to sort out a more detailed road program. Again, ride as many crits as possible, and mix these with short stage races and long one-day races to build your strength.

One of the greatest English-speaking 'cross riders of recent times, Steve Douce, overcame a life-threatening crash in a mountain bike race to defy the doctors and race again.

Most 'cross riders make excellent road riders, but it doesn't work both ways. The good fitness and bike handling common in 'cross transfer well to the requirements of road racing, but roadies riding 'cross usually suffer with their cardiovascular system — it makes them gasp! That is why so many continental roadies find cyclo-cross such an excellent form of training. It also improves their bike skills for the coming races on typical European roads ... many of which resemble 'cross courses themselves!

If you have come into 'cross from a mountain bike background, the chances are that you were drawn to it simply because you wanted to carry on racing off-road after the established off-road season had finished, and you probably even rode the early part of your 'cross career on the mountain bike until you realized that a 'cross bike was usually the faster option. Well, don't neglect the mountain-bike races during the summer. Many of them are like riding a two-hour 'cross, and the majority will subject you to the kind of terrain and effort that will make a 'cross seem like a ride in the park!

For the improvement of bike-handling skills and the training effect of racing for a prolonged time at a high heart rate, mountain bike races are simply unbeatable — you could never subject yourself to the same stresses through training alone.

The list of the world's best mountain bike racers is a who's who of 'cross riders, proving that the cross-over between the two sports is ideal. A rider like Henrik Djernis, the only rider to become world champion in both disciplines — three times on the mountain bike, and once on the 'cross bike — continues to be successful all year 'round.

His mountain bike season begins with a training camp in early March, usually two weeks spent somewhere warm getting long rides in on both road and mountain bike. This is followed by some early mountain bike races in late March and early April, to prepare for the first mountain bike World Cup events in mid-April.

In May, he rides a mountain bike stage race and some road races before another run of World Cup events in June. He takes a break in early July, maybe goes on vacation for a week, and spends the rest of July racing on the road.

Mountain bike races resume in earnest during mid-August, with a four-or five-week build-up to the world championships in late September. After that, it's time for another break, this one a little longer, before 'cross training starts in late October. By early December, Henrik is racing in earnest once again ... this time, on a 'cross bike.

Although it is a short 'cross season, just seven or eight weeks, he can still ride about 15 races, and hope to be reaching peak form in time for the world's in late January or early February.

The last stage in the build-up for the world's is a national team training camp in mid-January, two weeks prior to the world's. There, training takes place four times a day under the watchful eyes of the team coaches. Another break after the world's, and suddenly March has come around again!

How do you peak for a big race?

Physically speaking, this has already been explained in the preceding sections — by gradually decreasing the volume of training you are doing, and increasing the speed and intensity. This is a way of bringing you into form for a certain part of the season; in most cases, January and the national and world championships.

The rest of the skill involved in peaking is purely mental. You must concentrate on a certain number of races and these alone. All others are a means to an end — a step toward the next target race. Riders who treat every race identically, with the same amount of importance week-in week-out, simply don't rise to the occasion when it matters. Obviously, the form has to be there, but when it is, the difference between you and the next guy is in the mind.

Final preparations should be made during the week leading up to your big race. Resist the urge to fit in any last-minute panic training. If you haven't done it by now, it is too late; the best thing you can do is rest. Training should be light, with a session of intervals on Wednesday and Thursday just to keep you sharp. Spend some time making sure your equipment is in top condition. You can stick on new tires, but any other new equipment should have been fitted a couple of weeks previously and used to ensure it is trouble-free.

For the rest of your final buildup, don't change anything from your usual regime. Don't try any different foods that might not agree with you; carry on eating sensibly, with an emphasis on carbos as you approach the weekend.

You should be nervous, but if you know your preparations have gone well, you should be confident of performing to your full potential.

Training diary

When your season has been planned, you and your coach will have a good idea of the training you are going to do, and this should be logged in a training diary along with all your race schedules.

At the end of every day, you should note what training you have done, whether it varied from what you were supposed to do, how you felt, where you went, with whom and what the weather was doing.

If you performed a set of intervals, record the times and the recoveries. For circuit and weight training, note the weights and number of sets you completed.

You may find it a real drag writing everything down in this way, and you might not see much point to it at the time. It is only afterward, when you are trying to find the form you had last year, that you can look back to see how your preparation differed and how you were feeling.

Be honest with yourself when filling out your diary. If you felt terrible and went home after 20 minutes instead of finishing a three-hour ride, then say so. If you don't, you are kidding nobody but yourself.

For race days, include details of the weather conditions, how you felt during the race, the results and any other comments you have on your opponents — for instance, if any did not finish. As the season goes on, you will be able to see how you are doing compared to the other riders, and see any changes in their form, which you can use to your advantage in forthcoming races.

The other details to record are your waking heart rate (daily) and your weight (weekly). Note these at the same time of day and same day of the week. Also record the amount of sleep you had. Any variations to these figures can be symptoms of oncoming illness or overtraining, and you will be able to catch it early before it takes hold. ■

CHAPTER 8

LOOKING AFTER YOURSELF

Staying healthy as a hard-working cyclist is vital if you are to steer clear of injury and illness, which can ruin a season. The harder you train, the more susceptible you are to minor illnesses such as coughs or colds, as your resistance is much lower. A super-fit athlete is treading a tightrope between being on top form and being ill!

Common-sense measures — changing out of training clothes as soon as you get back into the house; dressing correctly while training; getting warm clothes on as soon as you finish a race — will help to reduce the chances of picking something up. You cannot pick up a cold virus from being cold and wet ... but you can pick one up more easily by being run-down, and getting cold and wet makes you get run down quicker.

Most viruses thrive in places where a lot of people congregate, usually in air-conditioned buildings with little fresh air; offices, public transport, bars, crowds at a concert or sports event. At any of these places your chances of catching a virus are higher, so try to avoid them where possible. This does not mean being a hermit, avoiding people at all cost — just use some sense, and if you are feeling a bit the worse for wear, don't hang around in a bar for a few hours!

The Belgian successor to the great Roland Liboton is Paul Herijgers; fake tan, Ray-Bans and shiny bikes make Paul the current king of style on the 'cross circuit. He was also world champion in 1994, which proves he can also ride a good race!

Work on your appearance — both yours, and your bike's. A clean, smart, shiny bike is nicer to ride, and you stand a better chance of noticing any problems because you will be able to spot them as you maintain it. Keep yourself clean, smart and tidy as well. If you are looking good, you are probably feeling good, and give a good impression to the public, spectators and sponsors. If you are sponsored, either individually or as part of a team, you owe it to them to look your best at all times.

Before the season starts, sort out any health problems you may have while you still have time. It is too easy to put things off once the season is under way. Make sure your visits to the dentist are up to date, and your anti-tetanus injections are current. When riding 'cross, you will suffer more than your fair share of cuts and bruises, so take precautions to ensure they do not develop into anything more serious.

You shouldn't train in the same clothing more than once, especially shorts and under-jerseys. Bacterial skin complaints, especially on your point of contact with the saddle, thrive on sweat; if they are allowed to develop, antibiotics may be required to clear them up.

Eyes take a hammering, too, being constantly subjected to mud, grit and water. Wash them carefully after a race; if there is any inflammation, use an eye bath.

By taking time to look after yourself, you can save time having to miss races or training due to something that could have been prevented. It takes much longer to get rid of a cold and its aftereffects than it does to prevent it.

As your cycling career progresses, you will be able to interpret what your body is telling you — whether you are doing too much, or whether you have an illness coming on. If you capture it early, you will have a far better chance of recovering quickly and getting back into your training routine.

Colds

Nobody is immune to colds and flu, and no matter how careful you are, chances are you will eventually get one or the other. Let's hope that it happens during the off-season, not two days before the national championships!

By keeping an eye on your resting heart rate, it is possible to catch a pending illness early, before the main symptoms appear. The normal precautions are total rest, keeping warm indoors and taking plenty of fluids. Never try to train with a viral infection. Evidence shows that you can do serious damage to your heart and immune system if you exert yourself while under the effects of a virus, so stay off the bike at all costs.

Most over-the-counter medications are for cold relief; they relieve the symptoms, but won't get rid of the virus. A lot of these products also contain substances which appear on the UCI's "banned" list; if you use one, and are subjected to a drug test, you could be suspended or even banned from the sport. If in doubt about any medicine, ask a doctor to take a look at the ingredients; if you're still unsure, do not take it. Better safe than sorry.

Meanwhile, when you feel something coming on, increase your intake of vitamin C and take soluble aspirin every four hours for the first two days, by which time you will have hopefully halted its progress. To relieve congestion, use steam inhalation with a preparation specific for the job such as Carvol, Vicks or Olbas. A few drops of the same on your pillow at night will also help breathing.

Any cold or cough that produces a highly colored mucus suggests a trip to the doctor, as it means a secondary infection has started. If so, a course of antibiotics is the only way to shift it. Always complete the whole course, even if you think the symptoms have gone. Afterward, eat plenty of live yogurt to replace the good bacteria in your stomach ... the antibiotics will have probably killed them off.

Injuries

From time to time, you may be injured in a crash, or develop sprains, strains and twinges simply through working too hard. It is important to try to get these complaints sorted out quickly before they develop into something more serious.

By warming up thoroughly and stretching regularly, a lot of injuries can be prevented; the traumatic ones caused by falls cannot, so look after them when they occur.

The standard treatment for an initial injury is RICE — rest, ice, compression, elevation. This helps to reduce the swelling and restrict the spread of bruising, both of which can slow down the healing process. As soon as possible after an injury, you should apply ice and bandage and raise the affected part. The first six hours after an injury are the most important, so act quickly. Also, never apply heat to a recent injury.

If pain or swelling increases, seek immediate medical treatment. If after your RICE treatment, the area still gives you problems, seek the help and guidance of a physical therapist, who will be able to tell you what you have done and give you a program of treatment and exercises to follow.

Never rush back into training after an illness or injury. Resume with light training, and gradually build up to the level you were at before. Take great care that you are getting plenty of rest and sticking to a good diet.

Massage

If you can get regular massage, then by all means take advantage of it, especially if hard training is making you tight and sore the following day. However, do not use massage as a substitute for your regular stretching, which can help reduce stiffness in an overworked muscle. Self-massage is well worth the effort, as you can do it anywhere ... and you don't need anyone else's help.

Start in a sitting position — in the bathtub is ideal — and begin at your ankle and work up. First will be your calf muscles between the ankle and knee. Use steady stroking movements upwards with gentle, firm pressure. Move next to the hamstrings at the back of the thigh, working in a similar way, and finish with the quadriceps at the front.

If you do it in the bath, the water and soap will reduce friction; otherwise, a light oil is ideal. But do not use so much that you cannot grip, and never use any heat-generating massage creams.

Nutrition

Food provides the fuel you need to run your body. No matter how hard you train, how shiny your bikes are, or how great is your will to win, if you don't provide your "engine" with the best-quality fuel, there is no way you can perform at your best.

The food you eat contains the following nutrients: carbohydrate, fat and protein. It also contains vitamins, minerals, trace elements, dietary fiber and water. No one food contains enough of each of these to meet the needs of the body fully; hence, the need for a "balanced diet."

The standard Western diet ensures that you get adequate supplies of all the above — and in the case of fats, significantly too much. However, you are not a standard Western person — you are a cyclist, and you need a bit more of certain things to cope with the raised levels of energy you have to produce.

The most important nutrient to you as a racer is carbohydrate. Carbs come in two forms: complex (starches) and simple (sugars). The best for you are the complex carbs, obtained from foods such as potatoes, bread, pasta, pulses, vegetables and nuts. In addition to the starch within these foods, there are also all the vitamins and minerals that are necessary to metabolize the carbohydrate.

Simple carbs are usually found in highly processed foods, in which the carbohydrate has been extracted from natural sources and broken down. Confectionery and sweet foods and drinks are usually high in simple carbs, and contain "empty calories" — energy, but nothing else.

Fat is used as the "low octane" fuel when riding, and is needed extensively as a fuel source, especially on long rides. But this does not mean that you need a high intake of fat. The traditional Western diet is too high in fat already, so you should eat as little fatty food as possible; your body will get all it needs from hidden fats in other foods.

Protein is another source of energy, as well as being required to manufacture and repair muscle. The best sources of protein are white meat, fish, beans, pulses, legumes, nuts and skim milk.

Carbohydrate supplements

But back to carbs: Tests have shown that you need very large amounts of carbohydrate during training and racing to replace the energy being expended. These amounts cannot be easily provided by food intake alone — the bulk is too much — so you can help matters by taking carbo supplements in liquid form during and after training and racing.

The recommended quantities of carbohydrate intake in grams, per kilogram of body weight, are as follows:

• Training: 0.5g carbs/kg body weight/hour.
• Refueling: 1-1.5g carbs/kg body weight.

For example, a 60kg (132-pound) person needs to consume 30g of carbs an hour during training, and 60-90g as soon as possible after intense training or a race, when the body is most receptive to refueling.

Now, you could try to take this amount in the form of food. But as a slice of whole-grain bread provides only about 10g of carbs, it would mean eating three or four slices an hour during training, and between six and nine slices straight after a race ... not very practical! So taking the carbs in liquid form is a much better idea — you have a bottle on your bike, and can rehydrate and feed at the same time.

The ideal carbo-drink mix is a pure complex carbohydrate prepared from corn starch. It is available flavorless and contains no sugars or salts to cause stomach upsets, and strongly concentrated solutions can be made and digested without problems.

Work out (as above) how many grams you will need, then take a look at the weather and decide how many bottles you will drink; if it is cold, maybe just a half bottle, if it is a hot day, two or three. Then simply divide the amount evenly into however many bottles you decide on. If you eat something as well, then take that into consideration. For example, a PowerBar, which is a popular form of energy in bar form, contains 40g of carbs.

You can use these high concentrations of drink mix if it is pure and unflavored; if it is flavored then you must never use it at concentrations higher than the manufacturers recommend, as gastric emptying is impaired and an upset stomach will be the result. If you use a flavored drink mix, then take a look at the label and see how many grams of carbs you are getting from the recommended amount of scoops, and either drink more bottles or supplement them with "real" food.

Riders who stick to the above guidelines for carbo feeding during training and racing have noticed great improvements in their ability to recover faster. They can train harder on successive days without feeling tired, and the results are obvious — better race results!

Vitamin supplements

Nutritionists tell us that a normal diet provides all the minerals and vitamins we require, and that vitamin supplements are simply a waste of money, as you simply flush them away. However, I think it is worth taking a vitamin/mineral supplement once a day just to make sure. And an iron supplement is also a good idea, especially for women.

A daily supplement keeps your levels topped up, and will not contain enough amounts of fat-soluble vitamins to cause you any problems. Take care, though: Don't think that because a vitamin is good for you, a megadose is very good for you. Large doses can be harmful.

Daily diet

Most people, especially athletes, are more aware of what they eat now than their counterparts were 10 years ago, and the basic guidelines for a healthy diet should be obvious to everyone. Reduce your fat intake; reduce sugar intake (including confectionery); increase complex-carbohydrate intake; and eat as much fresh, raw, unrefined vegetables and fruit as possible.

Reliance on junk food and fast food is usually the result of bad preparation or time management. It takes no longer to cook a bowl of pasta than it does to fry sausages, so if you are used to doing the latter, then change your ways!

Breakfast is easy; müesli or cereal, whole-grain toast, orange juice and yogurt are all quick, cheap, easy and full of the right things. At midday, whole-grain bread sandwiches with a low-fat filling are quick and nutritious. In the evening, pasta, baked potatoes, fresh vegetables, white meat or fish are again quick, easy and no problem to even the worst bachelor cook!

Between meals, eat fruit, müesli bars or PowerBar-style snacks, and replace fizzy drinks, tea and coffee with fresh fruit juice or plain water.

Don't worry about the occasional lapses — the odd burger or curry is not going to do you any harm. Just don't live on them every day.

Water

Water is probably the most important nutrient required by the body. It performs numerous important functions, temperature regulation during exercise being the one of most concern to athletes. Water also acts as the transport medium, ferrying nutrients, wastes and hormones around the body to and from various tissues.

Water loss through sweating of as little as 2 to 3 percent of body weight can seriously affect performance, so it is vital to keep hydrated at all times, especially after hard training. ■

CHAPTER 9

CYCLO-CROSS
INTERNATIONAL

hen you look back on the 1990s and consider who was at the forefront of world cyclo-cross during that decade, one name will leap to mind — Adri Van der Poel.

By the time the '96 world's came to France, Adri had already earned five silver medals and a bronze at the pro world's, and placed in the top five a staggering nine times. But time looked to have run out on him. Always the bridesmaid, never the bride, he seemed to be taking lessons from his father-in-law Raymond Poulidor — "the eternal second" in the Tour de France.

Adri Van der Poel's run of second places at world cyclo-cross championships came to an oh-so-sweet end at the '96 world's in Paris.

But Van der Poel was surely the most popular winner of a 'cross race ever when, in a freezing park in the Paris suburb of Montreuil, he outsprinted the two Italian favorites — former world amateur champion Daniele Pontoni, and the revelation of the 1995-96 season, Luca Bramati. Any other result would have been a travesty of justice, and as he dared his breakaway companions to come around him, I think there were even Italians in the crowd hoping that it was going to be Van der Poel's day!

Radomir Simunek
He has won every world title available, in a career spanning more than 17 years.

If it is longevity you are looking for in a 'cross career, then look no further than Radomir Simunek. The Czech rider won his first world crown in 1980 as a junior in Switzerland. He went on to win the amateur crown twice in the early '80s, and made up the full set by taking the pro title from under the nose of Van der Poel in 1991. He also has two silver medals to go with the set of golds.

Despite personal trials and tribulations, Simunek has appeared in the top 10 more often than anyone else over the past 16 years. In the mid-'80s, his career was said to be finished when he was diagnosed with a heart problem. He came back from this only to find himself imprisoned after two policemen died in a car accident in which he was involved during the early '90s.

The third rider to come "back from the dead" in the '90s was Mike Kluge. Winner on home ground in Munich in 1985, he repeated the feat two years later in similar conditions in Czechoslovakia, then went missing from the top echelons of 'cross until late January in 1992, when, after a five-week-long season he dominated the pro world's at Leeds to regain his crown.

Kluge is one of the very real characters in 'cross — he speaks his mind, plays to the crowd, and is either loved or loathed by all. A class act on a mountain bike, he won the World Cup in the early years of Grundig sponsorship. But his heart was still in 'cross, as he proved in Leeds and so nearly repeated the following year in Italy, when he finished second after a mistake on the

The resurgence of Mike Kluge brought a smile to the face of many a 'cross fan. An incredible athlete, on his day he is unbeatable; that day came when after years in the wilderness he captured the pro title at the Leeds world's in '92.

The greatest off-road racer in the world today, Thomas Frischknecht.

final lap cost him the lead he had held for much of the race.

He disappeared from view yet again in the mid-'90s, plagued by a stomach problem that wouldn't go away and proved impossible to diagnose. But in 1996, Kluge showed all the signs of getting back into shape ... just in time for the first mountain bike race at the Olympic Games in Atlanta, Georgia. But whether we shall be treated to his awesome talents on a 'cross bike again remains to be seen.

The 1990s saw the changing of the guard in international cyclo-cross; the older guys who had been around since the late 1970s all seemed to retire at once, and a new breed of rider emerged, one who would lead the way at 'cross during the winter, and again on a mountain bike during the summer.

The most talented rider to emerge in this decade was Thomas Frischknecht. Son of Peter Frischknecht, who finished second in world pro championship races during the 1970s almost as often as Adri would a decade later, "Tom Boy" won the junior world's in 1988; finished third in his first amateur world's in 1990; then led from start to finish to win his first senior world title in 1991 at Gieten, in the Netherlands.

Third, sixth and seventh in the following three years, he was the favorite in 1995 to win at Eschenbach, just down the road from his home in Feldbach on the shores of Lake Zürich. But a collarbone he had broken five months previous on the eve of the mountain bike world's was fractured again after an collision with a tree at a New Year's World Cup race in Belgium.

The main contender for the prize of "most talented rider to appear in the '90s looks to be the young French star, Miguel Martinez. Another lad with a famous dad — this time, a past winner of the polka-dot climber's jersey in the Tour de France — young Miguel finished third, eighth and fourth in his three attempts at the world junior cyclo-cross championship. During the '96 world's in France, he won the first-ever world's espoirs title for riders under age 23 ... at the tender age of 19. To rub salt in the wounds, he had also finished third in the senior mountain bike world's the previous year, dispelling the myth that racing off-road is for older guys.

The move to open racing in 1995 meant that the original amateur and pro class races at the world's became mixed into one "open" race. But this left a huge gap for riders just out of the junior category, trying to make their mark against riders 10 or 15 years their senior. So the espoirs category was born. A European-only championship on its debut in 1995 at Eschenbach in Switzerland, the first rainbow jersey was awarded in 1996 in the category that provides a stepping stone for younger riders.

It will be interesting to see if women's cyclo-cross makes the grade and becomes a full-fledged world title sport. The interest in women's mountain-bike racing has encouraged some countries to introduce 'cross races during the winter, but at the moment it seems the way is led by Great Britain and the United States, where numbers flourish. The more traditional European countries seem to be having a problem accepting that there are women out there who want to ride 'cross. But as more women take to mountain-bike racing, it cannot be too long before enough riders make it impossible for the UCI to keep ignoring the possibilities.

As the more serious countries like Switzerland and the Czech Republic continue to dominate the team results at world's, the nations with smaller 'cross programs, such as the United States and Great Britain, struggle to make their presence felt internationally.

With a new UCI-backed World Cup 'cross competition in place, in which results count toward world ranking points and world-championship starting positions, the nations that do not or cannot send teams to these races fall further behind. If they do send teams to the world's, they run up against the Swiss, French and Italians, who spend what equates to the entire racing budget of smaller federations on a single race … and any morale they brought with them soon deserts them.

However, Japan's entry into world cyclo-cross gives hope to all. Just a few years ago, the Japanese showed up completely clueless as to the ins and outs of the 'cross game. However, they watched and learned, and within a few years they reached a level at which they are competitive with many vastly more established nations.

If the Brits and the Yanks can take a page from the Japanese book, then maybe by the end of the decade they, too, can go home with their heads held high! ■

The numbers of women competing in 'cross is growing all the time, and it is just a matter of time before they have a world championship to compete in. Top mountain bike star and British 'cross champion Caroline Alexander races regularly during the winter to tune up her bike-handling skills for the summer months ahead.

World championship results

1990, GETXO, SPAIN.

Juniors.

1st	E. Boezwinkel	NL		41.51.
2nd	J. Chiotti	FRA	@	0.12.
3rd	N. Van der Steen	NL	@	0.16.
4th	J. Pospisil	CZE	@	0.23.
5th	D. Gil	POL	@	0.37.
6th	E. Vervecken	BEL	@	0.56.
7th	T. Kroll	GER	@	1.19.
8th	Y. Holwek	FRA	@	1.19.
9th	R. Jordens	GER	@	1.32.
10th	P. Flamm	GER	@	1.33.

Amateur.

1st	A. Busser	SUI		46.27.
2nd	M. Kvasnika	CZE	@	0.12.
3rd	T. Frischknecht	SUI	@	0.15.
4th	E. Piech	POL	@	0.18.
5th	E. Kuyper	NL	@	0.23.
6th	J. Blomme	BEL	@	0.27.
7th	R. Groenendaal	NL	@	0.30.
8th	F. Groenendaal	NL	@	0.41.
9th	D. Runkel	SUI	@	0.42.
10th	P. Hric	CZE	@	0.42.

Professional.

1st	H. Baars	NL		1.3.14.
2nd	A. Van der Poel	NL	@	0.05.
3rd	B. LeBras	FRA	@	0.05.
4th	F. Van Bakel	NL	@	0.05.
5th	P. De Brauwer	BEL	@	0.05.
6th	P. Richard	SUI	@	0.05.
7th	R. Simunek	CZE	@	0.09.
8th	K. Camrda	CZE	@	0.15.
9th	B. Breu	SUI	@	0.15.
10th	R. Honegger	SUI	@	0.52.

World championship results

1991, GIETEN, NETHERLANDS.

Junior.

1st	O. Lukes	CZE		45.47.
2nd	J. Pospisil	CZE	@	st.
3rd	D. Gil	POL	@	st.
4th	V. Vatlika	CZE	@	0.01.
5th	J. Ulrich	GER	@	0.01.
6th	J. Faltynek	CZE	@	0.04.
7th	M. Vrogten	NL	@	0.21.
8th	T. Bukowski	POL	@	0.36.
9th	R. Jordens	GER	@	0.45.
10th	P. Flame	GER	@	0.48.

Amateur.

1st	T. Frischknecht	SUI		50.19.
2nd	H. Djernis	DEN	@	0.23.
3rd	D. Pontoni	ITA	@	0.23.
4th	M. Gerritsen	NL	@	0.25.
5th	E. Kuyper	NL	@	0.30.
6th	T. Berner	GER	@	0.38.
7th	R. Thielemans	BEL	@	0.44.
8th	B. Wabel	SUI	@	0.44.
9th	R. Fort	CZE	@	0.54.
10th	P. Elsnic	CZE	@	0.58.

Professional.

1st	R. Simunek	CZE		1.4.22.
2nd	A. Van der Poel	NL	@	st.
3rd	B. LeBras	FRA	@	0.06.
4th	H. Baars	NL	@	0.24.
5th	W. Lambrechts	BEL	@	0.28.
6th	F. Van Bakel	NL	@	0.33.
7th	R. Honegger	SUI	@	0.37.
8th	M. Hendriks	NL	@	0.46.
9th	D. Arnould	FRA	@	0.56.
10th	C. Lavainne	FRA	@	1.40.

World championship results

1992. LEEDS, GREAT BRITAIN.

Junior.

1st	R. Hammond	GB		38.10.
2nd	V. Bachleda	CZE	@	0.20.
3rd	J. Faltynek	CZE	@	0.49.
4th	T. Bukowski	POL	@	0.55.
5th	M. Urban	GER	@	1.00.
6th	P. Perrin	FRA	@	1.10.
7th	R. Verhaegen	BEL	@	1.12.
8th	M. Zberg	SUI	@	1.22.
9th	J. Delbove	FRA	@	1.31.
10th	M. Elsnic	CZE	@	1.46.

Amateur.

1st	D. Pontoni	ITA		50.56.
2nd	D. Runkel	SUI	@	0.46.
3rd	T. Frischknecht	SUI	@	1.05.
4th	E. Magnien	FRA	@	1.11.
5th	A. Hubmann	SUI	@	1.13.
6th	A. Busser	SUI	@	1.38.
7th	P. Elsnic	CZE	@	1.38.
8th	R. Berner	GER	@	1.44.
9th	J. Arenz	GER	@	2.00.
10th	R. Fort	CZE	@	2.07.

Professional.

1st	M. Kluge	GER		64.36.
2nd	K. Camrda	CZE	@	0.18.
3rd	A. Van der Poel	NL	@	0.53.
4th	B. Wabel	SUI	@	0.55.
5th	R. Simunek	CZE	@	1.20.
6th	B. Breu	SUI	@	1.23.
7th	K. Kalin	SUI	@	1.32.
8th	M. Kvasnika	CZE	@	1.33.
9th	D. Baker	GB	@	1.40.
10th	D. De Bie	BEL	@	1.44.

World championship results

1993. CORVA, ITALY.

Junior.

1st	K. Ausbuher	CZE		45.18.
2nd	J. Friede	CZE	@	0.38.
3rd	M. Martinez	FRA	@	0.51.
4th	B. Blum	SUI	@	0.53.
5th	U. Steinmann	GER	@	1.05.
6th	E. Zucchi	ITA	@	1.26.
7th	G. Gommers	NL	@	1.31.
8th	M. Eberhard	GER	@	1.57.
9th	A. Mudroch	CZE	@	2.35.
10th	J. Zoli	ITA	@	2.35.

Amateur.

1st	H. Djernis	DEN		46.23.
2nd	R. Berner	GER	@	0.06.
3rd	D. Pontoni	ITA	@	0.30.
4th	O. Lukes	CZE	@	0.30.
5th	R. Groenendaal	NL	@	0.36.
6th	T. Frischknecht	SUI	@	0.40.
7th	D. Gil	POL	@	0.43.
8th	M. Janssens	BEL	@	0.46.
9th	P. Elsnic	CZE	@	0.51.
10th	U. Markwalder	SUI	@	1.08.

Professional.

1st`	D. Arnould	FRA		1.03.17.
2nd	M. Kluge	GER	@	0.09.
3rd	W. De Vos	NL	@	0.16.
4th	D. Pagnier	FRA	@	0.47.
5th	A. Van der Poel	NL	@	2.07.
6th	F. Margon	ITA	@	2.22.
7th	B. Wabel	SUI	@	2.33.
8th	P. De Brauwer	BEL	@	2.36.
9th	S. Bono	ITA	@	2.37.
10th	L. Bramati	ITA	@	2.46.

World championship results

1994, KOKSIJDE, BELGIUM.

Junior.

1st	G. Gommers	NL		39.48.
2nd	K. Ausbuher	CZE	@	0.24.
3rd	B. Berden	BEL	@	1.00.
4th	S. Nijs	BEL	@	1.24.
5th	D. Susemilch	CZE	@	1.27.
6th	D. Willemsens	BEL	@	1.40.
7th	M. Elsnic	CZE	@	1.57.
8th	M. Martinez	FRA	@	2.15.
9th	U. Steinmann	GER	@	2.16.
10th	B. Blum	SUI	@	2.17.

Open.

1st	P. Herijgers	ITA		1.0.38.
2nd	R. Groenendaal	NL	@	0.06.
3rd	E. Vervecken	BEL	@	0.37.
4th	D. Pontoni	ITA	@	0.49.
5th	A. Van der Poel	NL	@	1.10.
6th	C. Bonnand	FRA	@	1.25.
7th	T. Frischknecht	SUI	@	1.30.
8th	M. Janssens	BEL	@	1.35.
9th	R. Simunek	CZE	@	1.35.
10th	D. De Bie	BEL	@	1.40.

World championship results

Junior.

1st	Z. Mlynar	CZE		40.01.
2nd	G. Benoist	FRA	@	0.12.
3rd	S. Bunter	SUI	@	0.16.
4th	M. Martinez	FRA	@	0.18.
5th	P. Prosek	CZE	@	0.31.
6th	M. Nijland	NL	@	0.47.
7th	P. Dubacher	SUI	@	0.47.
8th	R. Zweifel	SUI	@	0.54.
9th	R. Pelgrims	BEL	@	0.59.
10th	F. Dall'Oste	ITA	@	1.06.

Espoirs (European Championships).

1st	J. Pospisil	CZE		52.09.
2nd	P. Halgand	FRA	@	0.24.
3rd	T. Steiger	SUI	@	0.49.
4th	P. Blum	SUI	@	2.12.
5th	D. Gil	POL	@	2.31.
6th	R. Hammond	GB	@	2.42.
7th	G. Gommers	NL	@	2.45.
8th	R. Korinek	CZE	@	2.51.
9th	C. Morel	FRA	@	2.59.
10th	C. Heule	SUI	@	3.07.

Open.

1st.	D. Runkel	SUI		57.44.
2nd	R. Groenendaal	NL	@	0.37.
3rd	B. Wabel	SUI	@	0.57.
4th	A. Van der Poel	NL	@	1.18.
5th	R. Honegger	SUI	@	1.26.
6th	P. Van Santvliet	BEL	@	1.43.
7th	D. Arnould	FRA	@	1.45.
8th	J. Ostergaard	DEN	@	2.01.
9th	D. Pontoni	ITA	@	2.11.
10th	E. Magnien	FRA	@	2.30.

World championship results

1996, MONTREUIL, FRANCE.

Junior.

1st	R. Peter	SUI		40.55.
2nd	G. Lejarreta	ESP	@	0.49.
3rd	G. Lapalud	FRA`	@	0.59.
4th	P. Frei	SUI	@	0.59.
5th	D. Derepas	FRA	@	0.59.
6th	J. Gadret	FRA	@	0.59.
7th	C. Trafelet	SUI	@	0.59.
8th	B. Wellens	BEL	@	1.23.
9th	M. Kern	SUI	@	1.36.
10th	D. Ticky	CZE	@	1.36.

Espoir.

1st	M. Martinez	FRA		46.57.
2nd	P. Blum	SUI	@	st
3rd	Z. Mlynar	CZE	@	0.04.
4th	H. Nijland	NL	@	0.04.
5th	K. Ausbuher	CZE	@	0.14.
6th	D. Sussemilch	CZE	@	0.14.
7th	D. Cioni	ITA	@	0.14.
8th	B. Blum	SUI	@	0.14.
9th	C. Morel	FRA	@	0.19.
10th	G. Benoist	FRA	@	0.25.

Open.

1st	A. Van der Poel	NL		56.12.
2nd	D. Pontoni	ITA	@	st.
3rd	L. Bramati	ITA	@	st.
4th	H. Djernis	DEN	@	0.09.
5th	E. Vervecken	BEL	@	0.09.
6th	E. Magnien	FRA	@	0.09.
7th	D. Runkel	SUI	@	0.21.
8th	R. Groenendaal	NL	@	0.21.
9th	J. Chiotti	FRA	@	0.39.
10th	B. Wabel	SUI	@	0.59.

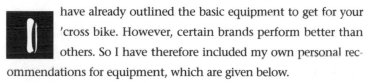

Recommended equipment for cyclo-cross

I have already outlined the basic equipment to get for your 'cross bike. However, certain brands perform better than others. So I have therefore included my own personal recommendations for equipment, which are given below.

Occasionally, the best bits for the job are hard to buy, either because they have been replaced by a different model, or because their availability is poor. Where this is the case I have tried to offer a suitable alternative, which, although it may not be as good, will be readily available at the bike shop.

Frame tubing

My all-time favorite frame is the Alan from Italy. Light, strong and smart, a new model "Top Cross" has recently been introduced. It has more clearance between the chainstays to accommodate the trend toward using tires wider than 28mm. Carbon fiber is available if you want something a little lighter and a lot stiffer ... but be prepared to pay the extra.

For steel frames, go for Reynolds 753 or Ritchey Logic.

Headset

A number of sealed units are now available to keep the muck out. Shimano make the best at the lower-price bracket, but be careful if you have had a Shimano and want to try something else — the stack heights of Shimano are very small, so the probability is that nothing else will fit your steer tube length. Campagnolo is really good, especially the Chorus model. If you have a frame and fork that will accommodate an "AHeadSet" design, this will be a good weight saving; in this case, the headsets from Dia-Compe or Cane Creek are good.

Bottom bracket

These take a hammering, so go one of two ways: Buy cheap sealed units that you simply throw away at the end of every season; or buy good-quality, preferably titanium models, which have replaceable sealed bearings that you can change when needed. You can save a lot of weight on the bracket, so go for a Syncros or something similar.

Seatpost

Mountain bike posts are light, but a lot of them don't have enough throw-back on the cradle, which means your saddle will end up being a long way forward. As long as the clamp is good quality, so the saddle doesn't move when you jump on, the make isn't so important. But get a seatpost long enough so there is plenty left in the frame. Campagnolo seatposts are quite short; Ritchey's are good and light.

Saddle

Use the lightest saddle you are comfortable on; Flite saddles by Selle Italia are the original lightweight cutaway style, and as good as anything. But San Marco makes lightweight, titanium-railed saddles that are a little wider and seem a little more robust.

Handlebars and stem

Always try to use the same make of bar and stem. If you are going super-light, make sure the clamp is the correct size for the bar. Cinelli makes the best bars — the new Eubios ergonomically shaped bars are great, and fitted to a Grammo titanium stem make a light, strong pairing. ITM and 3T are the other bars worth considering. And you can save weight by using a mountain bike-style stem, such as a Syncros, to save some weight.

Handlebar tape

Benotto is cheap, smart and easy to clean, but provides no grip at all. Cinelli cork ribbon is nice and comfortable, but needs looking after. Otherwise, just use Bike Ribbon.

Brakes

If you can find Weinmann 420 model cantilevers, they are the best. If you can't, then use Dia-Compe or Ritchey. As for levers, if you are going to use a gear/brake shifter combo, then I would go for Campagnolo over Shimano. They feel more positive, are less likely to damage after a fall, and look neater with the concealed cables. You don't need to go for the best model; Athena or Chorus work the same as Record, but are just a little heavier.

If you are going to use bar-end shifters, then Dia-Compe levers are good, as are Shimano.

If you decide to use a second pair of levers on the tops of the bars, use a mountain-bike lever such as Dia-Compe or Ritchey. The easiest way to work these is to use a second set of cables going into one cable hanger, both front and back. All you need to do is modify the front outer cable stop to accept a second cable, then make the hole in the clamp on the hanger slightly larger to fit the extra cable and adjust as normal. On the rear, if your frame has a cable stop built in across the seat stays, simply add another on the seat-post clamp bolt and run covered cable along the top tube to this extra stop. Secure the cable with tape or cable clips to the top tube.

Gear shifters

If you want to stick with bar-end shifters, then Shimano are the best on indexed setting.

Derailleurs

The only real choice is between Campagnolo and Shimano here; I prefer Campy, as they seem to last longer. Again, a mid-range model like Chorus or Athena works well. If you are a Shimano fan, then Ultegra is the way to go.

Cranksets

Use anything that gives you the crank length you want, and offers easy availability of 39- and 48-tooth chainrings. The latter are proving hard to come by nowadays, but TA makes a full range of rings to fit all popular cranks.

Pedals

Shimano's SPDs have the best action, but are too heavy. Either replace the steel spindles with titanium, or try a different pedal, like the new Ritchey.

Hubs/cassette

Go for whatever make you have decided on for gears and shifters.

Rims

Mavic makes the best rims: GP4 if you prefer the traditional shape in a tubular rim; CXP30 in a deeper aero' style. Use Cosmics if you have the funds available. For a clincher rim, Mavic Reflex are good, or try Campagnolo rims, which are great.

For composite wheels, Spinergy are the best at the moment, but save them for special occasions. Corima and Specialized are the best tri-spokes.

Spokes

Don't look any further than DT from Switzerland.

Tires

If you are going to use tubulars, then Clement are the best, particularly the new Griffo Largo, unless you can get hold of Dugast from France. Tufos are also good, with a tubeless design, which I like, but they might be hard to come by. For a clincher tire, try to find Specialized 34mm if you can; otherwise use Tioga Greyhound, or IRC.

Shoes

The fit is more important than anything; everyone I know loves Shimano M210 shoes, but I prefer Gaerne, Sidi and Northwave, as they have a little more give in the front for running. Like I said — shoes are personal! ■

INDEX